T0209151

PACIFIC
LST

PACIFIC LST

A Gallant Ship and Her Hardworking Coast Guard
Crew at the Invasion of Okinawa
Revised Edition

STEPHEN C. STRIPE

PACIFIC LST
A GALLANT SHIP AND HER HARDWORKING COAST
GUARD CREW AT THE INVASION OF OKINAWA

iUniverse books may be ordered through booksellers or by contacting:

iUniverse
1663 Liberty Drive
Bloomington, IN 47403
www.iuniverse.com
844-349-9409

Because of the dynamic nature of the Internet, any web addresses or links contained in this book may have changed since publication and may no longer be valid. The views expressed in this work are solely those of the author and do not necessarily reflect the views of the publisher, and the publisher hereby disclaims any responsibility for them.

Any people depicted in stock imagery provided by Getty Images are models, and such images are being used for illustrative purposes only. Certain stock imagery © Getty Images.

ISBN: 978-1-6632-5968-4 (sc)
ISBN: 978-1-6632-5969-1 (hc)
ISBN: 978-1-6632-6000-0 (e)

Library of Congress Control Number: 2024901450

Print information available on the last page.

iUniverse rev. date: 01/25/2024

CONTENTS

ACKNOWLEDGMENTS

I would like to thank Jonathan Wagner, Professor Emeritus of History, Minot State University in helping edit the manuscript and providing invaluable advice with this book. Thanking Mr. Scott Nelson the artist for the Illustration of the historic day that the 791 anchored in front of the USS Comfort, shot down the Japanese Val kamikaze and the Val and Zero sketches. My sincere gratitude and thanks go to the National Archives in their helpful endeavors in getting historical information to me. I would like to thank the United States Coast Guard in their help in providing information. To the men of LST 791 Association in answering questions in 2003 as to the events of their ship and providing artifacts, letters, pictures and their stories I give my utmost appreciation and thanks.

To my mother Fern Stripe-Bruhn (deceased 2013) wish to express my deepest affection and appreciation in providing historical context and stories of that time in the events that occurred on the home front during World War 2. I would like to thank Mr. George Hugh's son-in-law of Skipper Lt. Cdr. A. Duncan for contacting me and provided excellent memoirs of the skipper and many useful and interesting discussions. Also I would like to thank Lt. Cdr. A. Duncan daughters Isabel D. Hatchet and Madeleine D. Hughes for granting me permission to publish his memoirs.

And finally to my wife Stephanie I would like to express my most loving affection for the support she provided while I completed this project.

PREFACE

The following story of my father, his shipmates, the Skipper A. Duncan and their ship LST [Landing Ship Tank] 791 describes the conditions in which they existed and lived during World War Two. The ship and her Coast Guard crew existed for only 18 short months. They did yeoman duty in the South Pacific, most dramatically during the last great amphibious invasion of the pacific war, Okinawa. My father kept no diary, occasionally and rarely did he talk to me about his time in the Coast Guard. Some of his ship mates however did keep diaries and most of this work is based on them along with the deck log. Interviews conducted with surviving members, Fern Stripe-Bruhn and other historical references provided additional information. Lt. Cdr. Duncan wrote his memoirs down, therefore also became a source. This book is a tribute to all that sailed the amphibious navy in World War Two.

On July 25, 1942 the Coast Guard Headquarters authorized all naval districts along the coast to organize armed beach patrols, to operate as outposts and report all activities along the coast. The National Beach Patrol Division under the command of Capt. Raymond J. Martinson conducted the operation of its ten districts that mustered approximately 24,000 officers and men to patrol 3,700 miles of beach. Pairs of men armed with rifles, or sidearm's and flare pistols conducted the foot patrols. The pairing allowed one man to hold a suspect and another to go for assistance. Each patrol covered around two miles of beach. Patrols reported via special telephones placed at quarter mile intervals.

A Coast Guardsman, John C. Cullen, on beach patrol interrupted the Nazi Operation Pastorius on June 13, 1942, the Nazi attempt to put four sabotage agents ashore from U-202 off the coast of Long Island.

On June 3, 1941, five months before the Coast Guard transferred to naval command, an executive order President Roosevelt signed allowed Coast Guardsmen to serve aboard naval vessels. On November 1, 1941 under Executive order 8929 the Coast Guard transferred to the Navy for the foreseeable future.

Coast Guardsmen crewed 37 of the early LSTs serving in Navy flotillas. Thirteen LSTs went to the European theater of war and 24 went to the Pacific. In 1944 thirty six more LSTs had been commissioned and manned by Coast Guard crews. These composed the 29th Flotilla which took part in and impacted the Iwo Jima and Okinawa invasions. (Johnson, 1993, February) Indeed, besides manning 29 LSTs at Okinawa, Coast Guard men crewed 7 transports, two cutters, 12 LCIs [Landing Craft Infantry] and 1 sub chaser at the invasion.

Because invasion convoys often had been subject to air attack, almost all ships had to have some kind of antiaircraft defense, including transports and amphibious ships. Under combat conditions the LST had to beach under combat conditions to disembark men and material. The LSTs guns, offered antiaircraft and ground targeting to protect their cargo during disembarkation. After the initial beaching the LST, would then maneuver alongside another larger ship to load and embark additional cargo on the beach. This process could be repeated numerous times during a single landing operation. One LST repeatedly beached 90 times during its short 13 month war time career. When beaching could not be possible, pontoon causeways had to be employed between ship and shore. The LSTs also brought the pontoon causeways.

Cargo could be dangerous and lead to the loss of the ship. Army personnel on May 21, 1944 in Pearl Harbor had been in the process of unloading mortar ammunition when it exploded at 1505 hours on board

LST 353. LST's 43, 69, 179 and 480 had been moored alongside and sank. Two others also had been damaged. The explosion also destroyed other landing craft in the vicinity. 163 service men had been killed and 396 wounded in the West Loch Disaster of Pearl Harbor that day.

Two hundred and thirty one thousand men and ten thousand women served in the Coast Guard during World War II. One thousand nine hundred and eighteen died during the war, including 572 killed in action. At its height the Coast Guard manned 802 ocean going cutters, 351 naval vessels, 288 Army water craft as well as smaller vessels assigned to escort and port security. The Coast Guard also operated 165 aircraft. The Coast Guard returned to Treasury Department control on January 1, 1946.

GLOSSARY OF ABBREVIATIONS FOR COAST GUARD RATINGS AND RANKS

World War II Enlisted Ratings for Coast Guard and Navy were similar or the same.

BM, Cox	Boatswains Mate or Coxswain
GM	Gunners Mate
QM	Quartermaster
SM	Signalman
F, GR	Fire Control man, Gun Ranger
MM, WT	Machinist Mate, Water Tender Mate
B	Boiler mate
MoMM	Motor Machinist Mate (Motor Mac)
EM	Electrician Mate
Y	Yeoman
SK	Storekeeper
PhM	Pharmacist Mate
RM	Radioman
RdM	Radarman
TM	Topedoman
CM	Carpenter
Ptr	Painter
PM	Pattern maker

PhoM	Photographer Mate
CCS	Chief Commissary Steward
SC	Ships Cook or Officer Cook
Bkr	Baker
C	Cook
St	Steward
SSMB	Barber
SSMC	Ships Service Mates (cobbler, laundryman etc.)
SSMT	Tailer

Enlisted Ranks for Coast Guard and Navy are the same

S/a (SA)	Seaman apprentice
S/2	Seaman 2nd class
S/1	Seaman 1st class
PO/3	Petty officer 3rd class
PO/2	Petty officer 2nd class
PO/1	Petty officer 1st class
CPO	Chief Petty Officer
SCPO	Senior Chief Petty Officer
MCPO	Master Chief Petty Officer

Officer Ranks for Coast Guard and Navy are the same

Ens	Ensign
Lt. (jg)	Lieutenant Junior Grade
Lt.	Lieutenant
LtCDR	Lieutenant Commander
CDR	Commander
CAPT	Captain
RADM	Rear Admiral
VADM	Vice Admiral
ADM	Admiral

INTRODUCTION

The pacific part of World War Two was a Marine conflict, could only have been fought with amphibious ships and craft. Both the men, ships and landing craft of this amphibious force known as the alligator navy have received little attention or recognition. Without the landing craft, ships and the men on them, the war could not have been won. They enabled those who won the medals to fight the war. On many occasions the men of the alligator navy also fought and shed blood. Their job had been to deliver the troops, tanks and supplies to hostile beaches and if necessary defend those assets with their lives. All being ordinary men, they had no particular attribute that made them ideal for the task assigned to them. They knew only that they had a job to do and they did it. Finishing the job so they could return home to their families had been their goal. They should be called heroes and should be honored as such. What follows is a story of a ship and its Coast Guard crew, members of that gallant hard working breed.

Max E. Stripe a resident of Humeston Iowa enlisted in the United States Coast Guard early August 1942. Shortly after his enlistment he married Fern L. Shafer.

Emblem of the Alligator Navy (Stripe).

Max E. Stripe 1943 (Stripe-Bruhn, 2003-2010)

Many went on inactive duty until the training stations became ready to accept new recruits. Before being called up, he worked various jobs; including helping build an Army air base at Dodge City Kansas. The base had been used during the war for basic flight training for RAF [Royal Air Force] and Free French pilots. Later it was used for training of B-25 Mitchell and B-26 Marauder twin engine bomber crews as well as WASPS [Women Army Service Pilots]. It closed 31 July 1945.

In January of 1943 he had been called up to begin receiving basic training at Curtis Bay Maryland, just outside Baltimore. The tough, rigorous boot camp lasted six weeks. Early in the war boot camp had been eight weeks and by the end of the war it had to be shortened progressively due to war time necessities to four weeks. The start of basic included a physical exam for all the recruits with vaccine shots before being organized into platoons. Uniforms had been issued and each man was expected to stencil their names on each piece of clothing. Much like in other services each man had to be torn down mentally before being rebuilt into a Coast Guardsman by more experienced petty officers. In basic training they learned such skills as military bearing, basic seamanship, small arms, drill, physical training, and firefighting just to name a few. They had been issued the Navy's Blue Jacket Manual to study and expected to know it. Max didn't know how to swim when he entered the Coast Guard. Indeed, many of the men didn't know how to swim.

After basic training he had been assigned to Metompkin Island Station on the seaside shore from Accomac, Virginia. During his service there he walked beach patrol four hours on and four hours off, during which he had to punch time clocks placed along the route at prescribed times. This posting involved protecting the east coast and watching for spies and saboteurs being put ashore by Nazi submarines. During patrols they occasionally found crates washed ashore from torpedoed ships just off the coast. Servicemen and civilians would often find, then use the contents of those items that made it to shore from those ships sunk off shore. During one patrol crates of Blue Barrel soap had been found washed ashore and Max shipped three crates home. The soap was used by his family until the mid 1960s. Every eight days he received liberty for forty eight hours.

Fern, his wife, came out to Salisbury Maryland at the end of April 1943, rented an apartment for $35/month and worked as a waitress. Max hitchhiked the 44 miles to and from Salisbury to be with her on his free weekends. Max and Robert [Bob] Weaver got to know each other and became friends during boot camp and shore patrol. They talked Fern into moving in with Bob's wife Maxine in Accomac Virginia after Christmas. Maxine had a baby boy and having Fern live with her would help pay the rent, groceries and take care of little Bobby. Max's father passed away suddenly May 16, 1944. He had been notified by his sister, Hildreth, via telegram and had been able to get emergency leave to go home for the funeral. Max and Fern traveled home for the funeral, and then returned to Accomac. Shortly after that Max and Bob received orders that they had been transferred to Camp Bradford, near Norfolk, Virginia for amphibious training in the summer of 1944. Fern left to go home to Omaha July of 1944. She found a job at the Mead munitions factory packing 1000 lbs bombs.

Many of the crewmen formed lifelong friendships, as did their families. When spouses could be close to their servicemen stateside they found ways and money to do so. When circumstances dictated that men go overseas, their spouses often went back home and found employment usually in war industries.

*Max Stripe and Bob Weaver with little Bobby in Accomac
Virginia 1943. (Stripe-Bruhn, 2003-2010)*

Max and Fern at Accomac Va. 1943. (Stripe-Bruhn, 2003-2010)

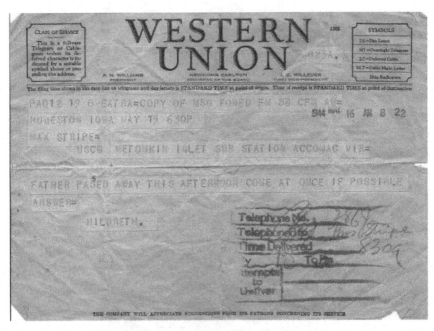

Telegram to Max about his father's death. (Stripe–Bruhn, 2003–2010)

Max Stripe home on leave in Humeston Iowa
1944. (Stripe–Bruhn, 2003–2010)

WHAT WERE THESE SHIPS?

The LST or Landing Ship Tank epitomized the war in the Pacific. Many are familiar with the more famous Higgins boats of which there had been three types, the earliest had been called LCP(L) or Landing Craft Personnel/Large. Designed by Andrew Jackson Higgins's from Columbus Nebraska, he built his factory in New Orleans. Almost all types had bow ramps which could be lowered to facilitate disembarking troops, and supplies onto the beaches. However, these small craft were not sea going vessels and had to be transported to the target invasion points on larger ones, such as LSTs and other ships.

The LST had been born in the United Kingdom from lessons learned from previous amphibious operations, such as Gallipoli, Turkey during World War I. Winston S. Churchill himself gave directions for the design and production of such ships. But, nevertheless the details for the manufacture had to be worked out within the United States. The LST had been a successful design as demonstrated by the last U. S. LST decommissioned in October 2002 had been the USS Frederick [LST-1184]. These ships had to be true amphibious transports with a length of 328 feet and a 50 foot beam, with their clam shell bow doors open and the ramp lowered, they could disgorge five hundred tons of supplies, twenty Sherman tanks or two hundred troops directly onto hostile beaches from the cavernous tank deck at one time.

The LST needed only three feet of water under its bow to get close to shore. Like a submarine it had a system of pumps and ballast tanks that enabled the ship to decrease its forward draft for such operations. Total capacity of the four ballast tanks was 398 tons. The forward tank had a capacity of 118 tons, with the port and starboard tanks having 40 tons capacities each and the stern tank 200 tons. When necessary these tanks could also be loaded with fuel oil so the ship could perform like a tanker. A LST could then winched itself off the beach by using a stern anchor that had been let go several hundred yards off the beach before landing, a technique called kedging. If a dock existed the ship could come up alongside and unload up to 2000 tons of cargo. In short the LST became the workhorses of the Pacific war carrying fuel, ammunition, troops, vehicles, tanks and any other cargo that needed transport to combat.

The LST had been one of the most versatile ships ever designed, beyond hauling cargo and troops, the LSTs could and did function as combat ships. Other variants of the basic design included hospital ships, torpedo boat tenders, battle damage repair ships, barracks ships, aircraft repair ships, landing craft repair ships, fighter direction tenders and aircraft carriers for launching L-4 spotter planes. Armaments on a typical LST included 20 mm and 40 mm guns used for antiaircraft defense and beach assault. But they could also be armed with 3 inch naval rifles and rockets. Optimum or maximum speed that an LST could attain was 11 knots, but its cruising speed was a paltry 9 knots. Because of these slow speeds at which these ships sailed, they sometimes had the moniker Large Slow Targets attached to them. Max recalled many years later a destroyer passing them and its sailors yelling to them to quit dragging their anchor. An LST could be built at an expected cost of approximately $1,500,000. At peak production one LST would be produced every 3.5 days. This ship truly made the United States Marine Corps amphibious.

CAMP BRADFORD

At Camp Bradford, Max, Bob with other Coast Guardsmen and Navy sailors trained for amphibious operations in the summer of 1944. During World War II over 160,000 Army and Marine troops trained for amphibious operations at the camp. Over 200,000 Navy sailors and Coast Guardsmen received instruction in operating various amphibious vessels there. Men, tanks and guns practiced loading and disembarking from LSTs, LSMs [Landing Ship Medium], LCVPs [Landing Craft Vehicle/Personnel], and other types of landing craft on beaches and rivers of the Chesapeake Bay. Thousands of men trained at the facility to man hundreds of LSTs. Camp Bradford did not have enough barracks to house all the men, so some had to be billeted in tents. Veterans of Mediterranean seaborne combat assaults provided the training. A mock up made out of wood and concrete of the top deck and bridge of a LST built on dry land, called the USS NEVERSAIL, was used in intense training. Most of the young trainees, still in or just out of their teens, and fresh from boot camp made up the majority. Others, like Max and Bob transferred in from other duty assignments.

During training many casualties inevitably occurred from

drowning, falls, accidental gun shots and all other assorted mishaps. This is especially true of young men who had the attitude of nothing can happen to them coupled with an adventurous spirit. Lt. Duncan, the future skipper of the LST 791, made the observation there: "In time one grew to accept casualties as an inevitable result of the extraordinary risks of the business, but when it was possible to reduce the risks it was wasteful and shameful not to do so." (Adams, 2002) He went on to say: "Far more formidable than all the other risks was the omnipresent menace of the sea itself. It was most deceptively dangerous when it was quiet and peaceful, for then it might either lash out in an unheralded storm and so trap the unwary or simply draw down into its fatal embrace the weak swimmer, the stunned, the drunken, the sick, or the careless. A growing familiarity with the sea's vastness made some of the men contemptuous of the fact that six feet of water could drown an able man and six inches a disabled one." (Adams, 2002)

Training at Camp Bradford covered everything a LST sailor needed to know from ship operations, landing operations, combat to emergency operations. The beginning organization of each ship or landing craft crew started at Camp Bradford. New crews had been housed together in the same Quonset huts. Officers and crews thought of their LSTs as fighting ships. On the eve of going to the shipyard in Pittsburgh to crew a new ship, the officers received orders. Each crewman's personnel jacket had been examined by skipper and executive officer.

Camp Bradford

"Just tell him it's because I'm an old fool," I said. "It's what they'll think anyhow. And if you want to expand on it you can add that I think the danger of some one being drowned here is greater than the offsetting pleasure of the swimmers." I watched the messenger withdraw maintaining a commendable effort to conceal the fact that the members of my prospective crew were not

5

the only ones who would consider me an old fool. I hated the decision the more because I felt that it should not have been thrust upon me. Either all of the formed crews should have been given swimming privileges or none of them should have. The hard experience of the preceding two years had taught me that the function of a Commanding Officer was to command, which inevitably involved hard and unpopular decisions, but there was no sense in forcing such a decision as this on a man with a new crew, especially with a new crew most of whom were softened by long stretches of coddling shore duty. I could hear Johnson now, who would come to me to complain that the best work could not be expected of the men in the deck division if they didn't feel that the Prospective Commanding Officer was duly interested in their comfort and happiness. Johnson would say it was a matter of morale. Johnson's conception of morale had been acquired at a base where dissatisfaction with the prevailing order had occasionally been expressed in private communications to congressmen, to the resulting discomfiture of those responsible. There might be trouble with Johnson. The amphibious training command should never have assigned him to the deck division.

I thought moodily that I should have been less abrupt with the messenger. I also thought of the manner in which my own convictions about the dangers of the sea had been acquired. We were beached now at the mouth of the Potomac, and it had been only a few miles south, at Lynnhaven Roads, that the sudden squall had caught the landing boats and drowned three men. It was two years and many thousands of miles ago that I had inventoried the effects of the one whose body had floated to the surface on the third day. Even to one who had not been very green and very junior the incident would have been pitiful and impressive. After that had followed the other casual accidents-- drownings, shootings, falls, and all the other categories--which marked naval and military life. In time one grew to accept them as an inevitable result of the extraordinary risks of the business, but when it was possible to reduce the risks it was wasteful and shameful not to do it. No one who had inventoried the childish effects of a young apprentice seaman could have had anything but *pity for the limited powers of self-preservation which might be expected of such a one, or fail to exert the utmost effort to avoid a situation which might overtax those powers.*

Far more formidable than all the other risks was the omnipresent menace of the sea itself. It was most deceptively dangerous when it was quiet and peaceful, for then it might either lash out in an unheralded storm and trap the unwary or simply draw down into its fatal embrace the weak swimmer, the stunned, the drunken, the sick or the careless. A growing familiarity with the sea's vastness made some of the men contemptuous of the fact that six feet of water could drown an able man and six inches a disabled one. Swimming was fine when properly supervised (as it would not be off training LST's), but to turn a bunch of careless kids loose in the water was making an unprofitable bet against the law of averages. There was a knock on the door. "Come in," I said, and looked around. "What can I do for you, Mr. Johnson?" It was not until the last evening that it happened. A messenger came in just as we were assembling in the ward room for supper and spoke to me quietly. I walked out rapidly, followed by my Executive Officer, and in a moment one of the junior officers came in with the news that a man was missing from the swimming party at the bow of the outboard ship. The officers were to proceed with supper without the Commanding Officer. Through my mind there passed reflexive images of confused shouting, tense interrogations, hasty musters, unsatisfactory reconstructions of the scene, and finally the hectic efforts to accomplish the empty recapture of the body. At the summit of these acts would be the ritual of investigation. If the officer in command of the training exercise had any confidence in the predictive value of past occurrences, he would not be too concerned about the consequences. The officers in the ward room dutifully proceeded with their suppers, and straggled out on deck. They congregated at the high, sloping bow and looked over at the place where the drowning had taken place. I t looked innocent enough in the fading light. According to the story going around, there was a treacherous tidal current which had developed on the other side of the ship and the boy had been taken out by it. Horton was

7

standing by me at the rail. "I hope our men have learned something from this. "I agreed, without indicating that I considered the hope well founded. Horton hesitated. He wanted to say something he thought indisputable, but was inhibited by the sound disinclination to do anything which could be considered flattering. Finally his innate kindliness and his confidence that he would not be misunderstood released the sentence. "They ought to be grateful." I continued to look at the beach. ""Gratitude has become one of the lost virtues." I started to say that it involved humility, but checked myself, and the two of us watched in quiet understanding as the colors of the evening softened into night.

The Crew

I entered the quonset hut and threw my hat on the bunk. "Here are our copies of the orders," I said to Horton. "There are some extras there." I looked at the personnel jackets which Horton had been sorting out and asked, "Did they give you all of them?"

"All except two," was the reply. "They're going to send two seamen second over at eighteen hundred with their own orders and jackets. We can quarter them in the Queen area for tonight."

"Well, plenty of things will come up tomorrow," I said regretfully. "They always do at the last minute. We're about ready." But I think "I'll be glad to get the men out of this place," Horton said with feeling. "So will I." I sat down on his foot locker. I paused, then spoke suddenly, as if making a reluctant confession which it was well to have over with as quickly as possible. "They're a sorry lot." I chose my words carefully. "Perhaps it's difficult, without a fuller standard of comparison, to assay just how sorry they are. It's not just that they lack spirit. Except in such a case as yours, or where a man has just come into service, the fact that he hasn't gone to sea by now shows how much spirit he has. Some of them are cowards. There is a percentage of them that will malinger before we get out of Pittsburgh, and some more of them will be in the hospital by the time we leave New Orleans. But the worst thing is that the

experience a lot of them have had in shore stations and around civilian war workers has given them the idea that they're cheated if they don't figure out an angle and get a free ride out of the war. "The fundamental trouble is that they don't want to fight. There are a few men in the crowd, but by and large the crew will have to be made to fight, and to the extent that we can do it, made to want to fight. It can be done, and we can do it, but it will be hard." I rose, and the sight of the personnel jackets inspired an afterthought. "This isn't just my idea. I don't have any figures on comparative discipline records, but look at the trails these men have left behind them: A.O.L., A.W.O.L., whiskey in possession, shirking duty, disobedience--the whole list. I thought of the great brawl at Key West." If there were just a few manly crimes recorded, I wouldn't mind quite so much. Thank Heaven for the few men we have who do look as if they might be able to stand up and be counted. There are some quiet ones that we'll hear from later on. It's a good thing. We'll need them."

Horton listened to this discouraging evaluation in silence. He realized that i t had been deliberately timed. Had it been given earlier, it might have prejudiced Horton, but on the eve of their departure for the shipyard an opinion such as this had to be furnished to the Executive Officer as a clear warning of trouble to come. "I wish we were going to sea tomorrow," he said. I'll say. In fact, I wish we had gone to sea the day we reported to this place. We'd all be better off."

On September 2, 1944 Max and Bob left for Pittsburgh, PA to join others to crew the new LST 791. The Dravo Corporation Shipyard at Neville Island Pittsburgh, one of five inland yards, had a workforce of 16,000 workers that produced a total of 145 LSTs during the war. Dravo Corporation produced primarily these types of ships during the war and contributed 2/3 of the Navy's fleet of over 1000 LSTs. 791's keel had been laid on 16, July 1944 and she launched on 26, August 1944.

Max and Bob arrived in Pittsburgh at 11 am on Sunday September 3. Carnegie Technical Institute dormitories provided the bunks for the fresh crews while in Pittsburgh until the ship made ready to sail. They spent their off hours going to U.S.O.s [United Service Organization], movies, dances, bars, restaurants and playing jokes on each other. Max recalled with much amusement one sailor's drunkenness when he came back from late night partying and tried to put his shirt on as pants. Also, when the crew got liberty in Pittsburgh, Fern rode a train for several days from Omaha to be with Max for those few days of liberty. While waiting for the ship to be ready to sail the rivers to New Orleans, the crew had their duties. They had to acquaint themselves with their new ship and home to be ready for overseas duty.

Launching of the 791: 26 August 1944 at Dravo Shipyards Neville Island Pittsburgh Penn. (Adams, 2002)

COMMISSIONING

The 791 partially commissioned and manned left Pittsburgh September 16 at 1800 hours. A Navy pilot navigated the treacherous Ohio and Mississippi rivers to New Orleans. No mast had been installed at Pittsburgh because of the necessity of passing under river bridges. During the inland voyage the ship ran aground on the Mississippi, making it necessary for repairs once they arrived in New Orleans. During the trip the crew practiced general quarters [GQ] or battle stations, along with performing routine ship operations; otherwise they had a pleasant trip through the heartland of America, arriving September 26 at 11 am at naval station Algiers in New Orleans. Moored on the port side to berth 3 and 4 at U. S. Naval Repair Base Algiers, the repairs accomplished and the ship outfitted for sea, including the mast being installed.

LST 791 was fully commissioned Wed. Sept 27, 1944 at 1400 hours on the tank deck as the main weather deck was undergoing authorized outfitting. Lt. Comdr. J. Wildman, E-V(s) U.S.N.R., the designated representative of the Commandant, Eighth Naval District and chaplain J. J. Travis U.S.N.R. [United States Naval Reserve] conducted the commissioning ceremonies. The chaplain read a prayer, and the Commandant's Representative read the directive, causing the national ensign and the commission pennant to be hoisted. Lt. Andrew Duncan Jr. U.S.C.G.R. [United States Coast Guard Reserve] assumed command according to the orders dated 2, Sept. 1944, Comphibtrabase, Camp Bradford, N.O.B. [Naval Operations Base] Norfolk Va. He then ordered the executive officer to set the watch at 1410 hours. After the commissioning party left at 1415 hours, the ship became part of LST Flotilla 29, Group 86, and Division 172. The crew consisted of 118 men; 7 officers and 111 enlisted men at the time of commissioning. The various homes of the crew members included most of the other states and representatives from the District of Columbia reproducing in microcosm the population of the United States. Other men would join the crew and others leave it at various times during its career as part of the pacific fleet.

Crew Photo at Commissioning Sept. 2, 1944. Max Stripe is the end man on the left 6th row. (Adams, 2002)

Officers of LST 791. 2nd Row: Ralph R. Bohrer, Charles J. Berlau, James E. Bradford, Dr. John H. Pritchett. 1st Row: Reed Adams, Harold T. Durkin, Andrew Duncan, Edward M. Horton, Wladislaw Zizik. (Adams, 2002): After April 17, 1945 to June 20, 1945 period.

TECHNICAL INFORMATION LST 791

LST 791's vital statistics provides one an idea of the operations of these magnificent ships. Two 900 h.p. General Motors Diesel 12 cylinder engines furnished the main propulsion. The ship carried a total of 188,000 gallons of fuel or 600 tons. At an engine speed of 275 rpm, or full speed of 9.8 knots, the average amount of daily fuel the 791 consumed ran about 2100 gallons. Crewmen living and working in the engine spaces, responsible for mechanical operation of the ship and engines called themselves the "black gang." The terminology of "black gang" dates from the time when most if not all ships were powered by coal fired steam engines. Coal dust would cover everything equipment and men turning them black. She could travel 24,000 miles at 9 knots.

The ship displaced 1,625 tons empty. Outfitted, the 791 carried two landing boats, LCVPs [Landing Craft, Vehicle/Personnel] slung from davits on the stern. Other versions of LSTs had four or more landing boats. Combat cargo capacity was up to 1900 tons. Fully loaded she would displace 4,080 tons. The water tanks held 85,000 gallons or 316 tons of fresh water. She had two water evaporators with a capacity of producing 2,000 gallons of fresh water per day. Lt. Reed Adams noted at the end of the war: "The old girl has made over a million gallons of fresh water." (Adams, 2002)

The ship provided berths for a normal crew of 116 men and 10 officers, plus 111 men and 19 officers as transients or casuals. Mess tables could seat 104 men below, 38 in crew's quarters, 66 on the starboard side and 21 in the ward room. The anchor weighed 5,000 lbs and had 60 fathoms [or 360 feet] of chain winched onto the windlass and capstan by a 20 h.p. motor. A 50 h.p. motor operated the stern winch that had its chain and cable attached to a 3,000 lbs. anchor. In earlier marks or series of LSTs, an elevator like apparatus moved vehicles between the main deck/weather deck and the tank deck as standard. LST 791 being a later mark had been fitted with a truck ramp that weighed 29,000 lbs. and measured 12 ½ ft. by 39 ½ ft. The ramp, when lowered allowed vehicles to be driven between the two decks and directly out the bow. When the ramp became flat and in line with the weather deck it supported a load of 60,000 lbs. plus loading impact or 38,000 lbs at 15 degree angle to the horizontal. The bow ramp weighed 24,000 lbs. She had four naval receivers and two transmitters, three army type receivers and transmitters and one RBO [recreational radio] receiver. They also possessed Radar and IFF [Identification Friend or Foe] equipment. Radar could detect high land 80 mile out, a low atoll 20 miles, aircraft at 16 miles and another LST at 17 miles.

Fighting the ship involved firing the mounted guns and beaching the ship to disembark vehicles and troops. Each gun crew operated in two sectors, termed primary and secondary. If an enemy aircraft entered the primary range of a gun crew; their obligation to first takes those targets under fire. This applied even if it involved shifting from another target outside its zone of primary responsibility. If the crew were not engaged in the zone of primary responsibility they then were obligated to fire on aircraft in their secondary zones.

The 791 armaments consisted of two twin 40 mm mounts with MK 51 gun directors, four single 40 mm mounts and twelve 20 mm guns. Twin 40 mm gun positions had been the stern and the bow. Single 40 mm had been just mounted behind the bow twin or ahead of the stern twin mount on both sides of the ship. The twin 40 mm's crew was composed of 7 men; a pointer, trainer, gun captain, two first loaders and two second loaders. A single 40 mm crew composed of 5 men, just lacking 2 additional loaders, but otherwise had the same positions as the twin. A 40 mm had a maximum range of around 11,000 yards and effective range of 3,000 to 4,000 yards. The 20 mm's mounted on both sides of the bridge, on the stern and bow behind the 40 mm and sometimes along either side of the main deck. 20 mm mounts had been crewed had 3 to 4 men and had a maximum range at 45 degree elevation of around 5,000 yards.

40 mm guns had three types of ammunition. H.E.T. or High Explosive Tracers was used mainly against aircraft. A.P.T. or Armor Piercing Tracer directed against tanks or pill boxes ashore. A.P.T. also had on its menu submarines. The first shell loaded into 40 mm guns in case it became necessary to fire through the muzzle cover in an emergency usually consisted of the B.L.&P or Blind Loaded and Plugged round. All 40 mm ammunition had packed 4 shells to a clip, four clips to a can. A shell weighed 4.75 lbs, the projectile weighed 2 lbs, and a clip of four weighed 20 lbs. So the loader of a 40 mm gun had to be strong and have endurance during battle. Three types of 20 mm ammunition used, H.E.I. or High Explosive Incendiary, H.E.T. or High Explosive Tracer and B.L. &P. A complete 20 mm shell weighed ½ lbs. and the projectile weighed ¼ lbs. They came packed 180 rounds to a can. The clips fed to the gun and each clip had 57 rounds in a magazine. A full magazine weighed 60 lbs. Total 40 mm stowage capacity including magazines consisted of 15,400 rounds or 3,850 clips. The ships allowance, however, only consisted of 12,000 rounds or

3,000 clips. Forty millimeter gun had a theoretical rate of fire of 120 rounds per minute or 30 clips per minute. Total 20 mm ammunition capacity for an LST consisted of about 108,000 rounds; however the ships allowance made only 48,000 rounds. Twenty millimeter gun had a practical rate of fire of 228 rounds per minute or four magazines per minute. The 20 mm's fire was less effective against aircraft, especially kamikazes than the 40 mm's.

SHAKE DOWN

After repairs with new screws installed due to grounding on the river voyage and outfitting, the ship left for St. Andrews Bay, Panama City, Florida on October 8 arriving on October 10, 1944 at 2 am. There she underwent a shakedown cruise and more training. This included swinging the ship to compensate the compass, practicing General Quarters, docking drills, target practice on both aerial and surface targets, beaching assaults with kedging, simulated dive bombing response maneuvers, operating the small boats, practicing emergency procedures, tactical maneuvers and degaussing [demagnetizing the ship to protect it against magnetic mines].

The dog Soogie destined to be the ship mascot had been picked up at the shipyard in New Orleans. A gunner's mate appropriated her from the shipyard superintendent and smuggled her aboard under his jumper after dark one night. The little canine was a small chubby white soup hound standing about 8 inches high. She had to be a good sailor as she got seasick only once.

On October 22 after eight days they left Panama City at 4 pm for New Orleans, arriving there at 8 pm with liberty being granted the following day. There they loaded five LCT [Landing Craft Tank] sections on the weather deck and quartered LCT 850 and LCT 1250 crews. Lt. Terrance F. Mc Nulty assistant surgeon USPHS [U. S. Public Health Service] reported aboard on the 27. Ballast tanks had been filled with bunker C oil. They left October 31 for the Naval Ammunition Depot in Mobile Bay and arrived at 6 pm on November 1. While in Mobile they loaded 850 tons of ammunition along with thirty gallons of milk and three hundred pounds of bread for the mess and left November 3 at 7:45 am. November 5 at 4:15 pm they sighted Cuba to port and at 8 am on November 8 they observed a blimp doing submarine patrol.

November 9 the mountains of the Canal Zone became observable at 12:20 pm by the crew. They crossed the sub nets at 5 pm protecting the entrance to the canal. The water front at Coco Solo Naval Base in Limon Bay and Colon had been described by Howard Riley "as looking like something out of a Dotty Lamoure movie." (Adams, 2002) They had to wait their turn among other ships at anchor to go through the canal. Late afternoon on Saturday November 11th they passed through the Gatun Locks. During the passage through the canal the crew saw scenery of the shoreline dense with foliage coming down to the water edge. Howler monkeys, sloths and birds of every size, shape and almost every plumage conceivable could be seen from the weather deck in the jungle and at the water's edge. At 2205 hours they entered the Pedro Miguel locks and finally cleared the Miraflores locks at 2400 hours.

Miraflores Locks Panama Canal, 2009, (Stripe Photo, 2009)

Liberty had been granted in the Canal Zone. It has been said that the two most common professions in the zone had to be bartenders and ladies of the night in the more seedy and frequented districts. Some of the crew visited those bars and brothels to imbibe of those pleasures. In the words of one crewman, they "got tight". (Weaver, 1943-1945) All returned from liberty on time except for six crewmen, who had been returned by the Shore Patrol. One attempted to bring liquor onto the Naval Base and was caught.

November 12 they left the Canal Zone at 10 am, traveling in the company of LST 726 and LST 940. They continued training with signal drills and test fired the Browning machine guns, with the small boat crews being instructed in the use of those weapons. The ship arrived in San Diego California and moored to the port side of LST 940 at the head of Mole Pier U.S. Naval Repair Base at 1100 hours on the 24. They had been fueled by the Navy oiler barge YO-52 with 29,668 gallons of fuel oil. Ships stores had been taken on board and the crew had been paid. R. D. Peetz S2c, M. E. Tibbals S1c, and M. Dime F1c reported aboard for duty on the 28th. Earl, Morris H. CMoMM and Charles B. Graham GM1c had been transferred to USCG Patrol Base for change of duty. McNulty was transferred back to the Coast Guard Operating Base back at Mobile Alabama. Liberty had been granted for overnight on the 25. Despite the thousands of service men San Diego had not been much of a liberty town. Some of the men went down to Tijuana, but didn't have much money or time to do any damage. The next port of call would be Pearl Harbor for which they weighed anchor at 11 am on the 30 of November.

During the trip to San Diego they sailed in relatively calm waters. Once in the open Pacific on their way to Pearl they had entered a war zone. LST 791 in company with LST 940 set sail without escort. Two days out they sighted a carrier and her destroyer escort. Another LST 756, joined up with the small convoy four days out. The 2300 miles from San Diego to Pearl took 12 days. On December 9 radar sighted the island of Maui at 1320 hours and they arrived in Pearl Harbor on the 10th of December.

Interim Menagerie Report

While there are some narrow-minded souls who do not appreciate our friends of the animal kingdom, even as pets for children, sailors and soldiers are men of great heart for a homeless animal. The result is that as of yesterday we had aboard three dogs, three monkeys, and one parrot. In routing some of the innumerable orders and edicts that guide our conduct I absentmindedly turned over to old Sawbones (also known as Cowboy) an order concerning animals. I hadn't read it (if I read everything how would I get time to write letters) but the Doc came in later and said we were ordered to kill the parrot - -all parrots, that is. Chet (Admiral Nimitz to the more formal) might not have known about the parrot, but the Doc sadly advised me that there was some danger

of parrot fever. Well, there seemed no out, so O'Malley, S2C, who owned the parrot was duly advised. Upon the little stand he had built for his feathered friend there is today an imitation flower, surmounting the following sign:
IN GRATEFUL MEMORY OF ONE WHO GAVE HIS LIFE THAT OTHERS MIGHT LIVE.

Ship's mascot playing with a monkey on the deck hatch. (Adams, 2002)

HAWAII

Liberty granted to the crew on the 12, one section at a time. The SP's [Shore Patrol] had a reputation of being tough, with no sense of humor. Too many sailors, soldiers, airmen, and marines with too much time, money and no place to go to spend it made for interesting and sometimes amusing adventures. Liberties lasted from 0830 hours to 1900 hours [6:00 PM]. Everyone, including civilians, had to be off the streets at 2030 hours due to curfew. Curfew enacted the day Pearl Harbor had been attacked on December 7, 1941. Honolulu being very crowded induced some of the men take a bus outside of town. Riley and his fellow shipmate Charbonnet boarded a bus and made it to the famous beach Waikiki. Reportedly Max and others also made it there to swim in the surf or sunbath. Riley described Kalaheo Avenue as the principle street in Honolulu as being wide and lined with coconut palms. Walks with fences covered with flowering vines decorated the avenue. At Waikiki they rented some swim trunks and took a dip or sun bathed and watched the girls. Riley stated: "In this, however, we were disappointed no more than two or three appeared and they were well convoyed by a full regiment of army officers. While we were just lying there in all our bachelor glory." (Riley, 1943-1945) The men had four liberties in Hawaii, part of each one they spent at the beach. Some tried to surf, but again as Riley said: "It takes an artist to navigate one of those damned things." (Riley, 1943-1945)

After the beach they often had lunch at a place like the Waikiki Tavern. The establishment being described as a regular restaurant with a couple of sides missing offered food, drink and entertainment. Birds landing on the floor to eat the crumbs fallen from the tables. At these taverns they would sometimes see what could only be described as a character out of a novel about the islands. Riley said: "A man approaching middle age, mostly bald and slightly bleary eyed and with that very red complexion caused by the prolonged use of alcohol, especially the nose, lined with broken veins. When we spoke to him he talked like a very well educated and cultured person. Truly the broken down intellectual type who had ended up in the islands playing the piano for whatever he could get, [sign said: Eddie Manly at the Piano from noon to five daily]." (Riley, 1943-1945)

The Royal Hawaiian has been described as the "more beautiful structure anywhere on earth." (Riley, 1943-1945) Architecture of the building could be pictured as a cross between Moorish and oriental styles, with the whole complex radiating a pinkish color surrounded by a deep grove of palms. The interior defied description where all the walls had been paneled and intricately designed. Naval authorities used it as a rehabilitation center. Some of the men took tours of the country side or ended up in U.S.O.'s. Others visited one of many cathouses in Honolulu, which often had lines of customers extending down or around the block.

The 10th saw Lt. Commander F. Allen the navy pilot come aboard to navigate into the harbor and moor the starboard side to LST 84 at Tare Seven. On the 11th Commander Culver USCG came aboard to inspect the cargo. On the 12th at Pearl a Yard Crane came alongside and unloaded the 5 LCT sections. Officers and crews of LCT 850 and 1250 had been disembarked on the 13th. On the 14th they had moved and moored at the U.S. Naval Ammunition Depot Berth W 4, where unloading of the cargo of ammunition commenced and would be completed on the 19th. At 1255 hours on the 19th they traveled down the channel in the West Loch and moored the port side to Berth B 16 and Navy Yard workers transferred to LCT 1250 their full allowance of ammunition, which had been carried as freight. Riley thought: "Nobody is sorry to see that go. Just like riding around on a time bomb, wondering if and when it's going to go off". (Riley, 1943-1945) The skipper, however, thought ammunition as being good cargo. The reason being it would always stow well and does not shift. It is heavy and sets the hull down in the water, making the ship ride well. The cargo is clean and when the ship had ammunition aboard they didn't carry personnel. Ammunition is generally inert unless it is fused. Also, if the ship is flying the red pennant other ships have a tendency to avoid you. (Adams, 2002) On the 20th the LCT 828 was placed aboard by crane onto the weather deck. Her navy officer and crew reported aboard.

The L.C.T. being a type of large craft that that could carry tanks onto the beach. These craft had to be hoisted onto the main deck of the LSTs by cranes. U.S. operated primarily Mk V and VI L.C.T.s, which had a length of 117 to 119 feet long by 32 feet wide and displaced 133 to 143 tons respectively. Each craft had 3 foot drafts and could carry 3 to 4 tanks or 150 tons of cargo to the beach and unload via a bow ramp. Cruising speed of 8 knots powered by three 225 h.p. diesel engines made them slow, but the advantage of speed was not necessary for beaching operations. Crews consisted of 1 officer and 12 enlisted men. LCT 828 was a type VI. Four other smaller landing craft, 2 LCVPs [Landing Craft Vehicle Personnel] and 2 LCMs [Landing Craft Mechanized], had been placed around the LCT. The LCM had been similar to the LCVP but larger and could carry one tank, 60 troops or 60,000 lbs. of cargo.

On the 21 fuel oil was discharged from two ballast tanks. A rectangular pontoon had to be made of reinforced steel measuring 5 ft by 5 ft by 7 ft and weighed one ton so it could support a ten ton load. A causeway consisted of two pontoons welded together side by side for the width and 15 sections welded on for the length, with connecting pontoons at each end. Two of these huge pontoon causeways running two thirds the length of the ship had been secured to the sides, making the whole ship look incredibly unwieldy. Sometimes pontoons welded together had a motor and propeller added to make them motorized barges, which LSTs carried the same way as causeways or on the weather deck.

December 23 they left the harbor at 9 am for Kewalo Basin Dock Waikiki to load for combat. On the 25th they celebrated Christmas with Max being thrown in the ocean as part of those festivities. The Captain of the Port Lt. (jg) John Mahlmann came aboard to investigate the running of a "jitney" [a small vehicle used as a taxi] belonging to the NSD [Naval Security Detail] off the pier into the water. Upon questioning of the ships company concerning the matter F1c C W Blair confessed to accidentally driving off the pier on that date. He was put on report. During Captains Mast for the infraction he was given a reprimand.

A unit of Sea Bees [C.B. or Navy Construction Battalion] came aboard and part of an army tank battalion, consisting of trucks, jeeps and armored cars were loaded and stowed on the 27th. Some other army and navy personnel had been quartered as well. Lt (jg) Frank Ruppert transferred off the ship. The 29th they set sail for Kwajalein atoll. They didn't stop there, but continued on to Eniwetok atoll. On first of January 1945 they blew the ships whistle for New Years. At 0800 hours on the 4th they crossed the International Date Line, which made it the 5th of January.

WAR ZONE

During sea voyages it is mostly boredom. A space between the bow doors and the ramp existed where crewmen would go to secure the bow doors with clamps and turnbuckles after closing. Max had been known to have taken snoozes in that space in the bow, the constant splash against the bow doors had a somnolent effect. Routine duties at sea included maintenance of the ship. In a humid salty sea environment rust sets in early and aggressively on a steel structure like a ship. This requires constant scraping and painting of the ship. Max recalled years later: "It seemed as though all we did when at sea was scrape and paint." (Stripe-Bruhn, 2003-2010) Watches would change on a prescribed schedule, usually four hours on watch and eight hours off. Bob Weaver had the 8 to 12 watch at the wheel on January 5th. On the 6th the captain held an inspection in the morning and the men rested on the afternoon. An inspection of the ammunition magazines was generally held every day as was the cargo, with conditions usually reported as dry and normal. The ships sprinkler system would be tested on a schedule. Every Sunday that could be observed a chapel was held on the tank deck. A weekly captain's inspection of the ship had been part of the routine on a weekly basis. Starting on the 7th they started gun watches and going to general quarters at sundown. General quarters [G.Q.] occurred at sunrise on the 8th. General Quarters and firing practice was held on a regular schedule. Zig Zag course was maintained hoping to fool submarine torpedo aiming in the hostile waters of the Pacific. On the 9th of the month, Thomas J. Lane MoMM1c extended his enlistment for 2 years.

They arrived at Eniwetok on the 10th at 0800 hours. There had been a lot of shipping there, mostly consisting of freighters, tankers, a few destroyers and several LSTs. At Eniwetok a major battle had been fought by the 106 Army Infantry Regiment and the 22nd Marine Regiment in February of 1944. The scene when the 791 arrived was that of hardly any trees standing, just stumps. It is a large coral atoll of 40 islands in the Marshall group. As on Eniwetok itself major combat occurred on Engebi islet and Parry Island. The crew described the islands as nothing more than oversized sand bars. An air strip and a few huts only existed on the Eniwetok Island. Prescott S1c had been injured by a fall from a 40 mm gun tub and was attended by Captain Rosner of the U.S. Army. He was subsequently transferred to the Naval Hospital on Eniwetok Island. While anchored at Eniwetok they heard that Luzon had been invaded. It was there at Luzon that they thought they might see action, but no one was anxious for it. Another idea going around the ship had the idea they would be involved in the invasion of Formosa and the China coast. Such is life aboard wartime LST, full of rumors.

Bob Weaver and his small boat took a liberty party to Parry Island 10 miles away for a beer celebration on the 11th. On the 13th Riley with others went ashore to play ball on the beach and others swam in the surf. Bob spent a lot of time in the small boat and complained of being wet most of the time. The landing craft of which Bob Weaver became one of the men crewing the two aboard the 791 had been used for ferrying men, supplies between ships and shore. The L.C.V.P. or Landing Craft

Vehicle Personnel was an updated version of the famous Higgins boat. It was 35 ft long by 10 ft. 10 in. wide and weighed 15,000 lbs. These craft had been made of wood with a steel bow ramp and cruised at a speed of 12 knots. Being capable of delivering 36 troops or 8,100 lbs of cargo to the beach, including small vehicles had been the reason for it being carried by transports. They had been armed with two .30 caliber machine guns. Generally the landing craft had 3 to 4 man crews, a coxswain who commanded and drove the boat, a motor-mac the machinist who operated the engine and maintained the boat and one or two seamen who helped tie up the boat, operate the ramp and perform other needed duties such as manning the weapons. As they were making preparations to get underway a fire alarm sounded for a fire of undetermined origin in the lucky bag on the tank deck, but was quickly controlled. On January 14 they shoved off for Babelthaup and Leyte in the Philippines.

Eniwetok

There are many lagoons in the Pacific and Eniwetok seems to be fairly typical. You have heard of peaceful lagoons. So have I, but I haven't seen one yet. Maybe in another season, but in January, when we were there for nearly a week, it was almost constantly rough. The trade winds blow with no hindrance across the vast spaces of the Pacific and there is little daily change in their direction or intensity. A lagoon is merely a shallow place in the ocean, bordered in places by a narrow island amounting to nothing more than a glorified sandbar. On the largest island we usually put an airfield, or air strip. In some places there are practically no facilities ashore, everything is afloat. Supply ships, repair ships, oilers, even water ships, take care of our needs. This ship has not been alongside a dock for well over three months - - not since leaving Pearl.

At first sight Eniwetok scarcely seemed worth bothering with, let alone fighting for. But it is useful as an anchorage. It is large, and offers a little shelter for afloat maintenance and supply which could not be handled underway in the open sea. The air strip is useful. Kwajalein seemed much same. We went close by there, but we did not stop. You go through the passage and anchor, keeping clear of the coral heads. The lagoon may be as much as 60 miles across, though that is an outsize and most of them are much smaller. The islands of the characteristic Central Pacific lagoon seem low, seldom rising more than a few feet above s e a level. The unfortunate individuals who are stationed on these islands are also low. It is a monotonous existence. One may swim, or walk around the island and gather coconuts and seashells, or drink a few cool ones at the officer's club, but facilities are not elaborate. There are usually movies, but in all my time overseas I have never seen but one good movie or heard of but one good one being shown. Most of them are old grade B or C movies. Have seen two movies since October) (The one good one was "Random Harvest" which I saw on a transport at Oran.) So much for lagoons. They are scrub islands with a hole in the middle.

Trouble was expected on this run, but thankfully it would prove uneventful. One G.Q. called at 1300 hours and described as a dummy run. Someone got trigger happy and started shooting at one of the other ships in the convoy. They stood battle stations for about twenty minutes, and then went back to bed. On January 20 they worked topside getting ready for a Captains Inspection that had been turned over to the first officer. The convoy split at Ulithi, and they arrived at Babelthaup in the Palau group on the 22, at 1100 hours. Babelthaup the biggest island in the Palau group was still held by the Japanese and Kossol Passage lies just north of the island. They anchored in berth 78 at Kossol Roads. Allied planes had airstrips on the surrounding islands and would from time to time bomb and strafe the island. The enemy just couldn't seem to get planes into their field. Occasionally ships lying offshore would be fired on by a frustrated enemy. The skipper commented: "Out here you get used to having Japanese all around on bypassed island bases. Wotje, Yap, Babelthaup, Bougainville, some of the Philippine islands-all of these have Japanese on them. They are still ready to fight, too." (Adams, 2002) They stood gun watches when they arrived, as an enemy garrison only stood about three miles from them.

Kossol Passage

This is merely a shallow place in the ocean, slightly protected by a reef. We have a couple of small islands in the Palau group, but the biggest, Babelthuap, is still held by the Japs. Kossol Passage is just north of that. So: Looks crazy, doesn't it? Our planes bomb and strafe the big island from time to time. It's very leisurely. The Japs can't seem to get planes in to their field there. We have one or more fields on the little islands. we lie too far offshore to be shot,at. My chart is oversimplified. NEWSWEEK'S account of all this is more intelligent, but may not be right at hand.

Out here you get used to having Japs all around on bypassed island bases. Wotje, Yap, Babelthuap, Bougainville, some of the @Philippine islands – all of these have Japs on them. They are still ready to fight, too. So we just go by and don't get too close. I have an idea that for a good many years people will be just going by some of these islands. That would suit me all right. Many have no value even now. When the Empire is gone, they will be no menace at all.

Bob got three letters on the 24th during mail call, and that afternoon he went back to small boat duty. Mail is a big part of moral for servicemen overseas. The men had access to writing materials from the ships stores, but occasionally they would use any handy scrap of paper to write letters home, such as the ship's menu. All mail processed by the military underwent severe censorship as to any clue to location and mission. Therefore, most communication written by the crew had to be general, emotional and not very informative.

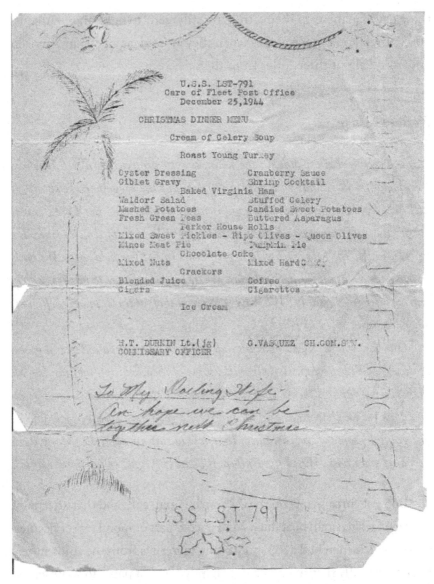

*Letter Max wrote to Fern on Christmas menu
for 1944 (Stripe-Bruhn, 2003-2010)*

On the 26th the crew was kept occupied with ship handling drills around the harbor in preparation for an anticipated combat beaching. The next day they prepared to get underway and hoisted the small boat aboard and secured for sea. On the 28th they set sail with a small convoy escorted by two destroyers and a destroyer escort. Following day they joined up with another convoy, making up a total of 64 ships. At 0300 hours on the 30th they went to G.Q. because a sub had been sighted off their starboard beam. The next day another G.Q. sounded at 1300 hours for an unidentified plane, which turned out to be an allied plane. At 1100 hours on the February 1 they sighted land and anchored five miles off Capines Point Samoa at 1900 hours. Staying only overnight they then again weighed anchor and headed for Leyte.

Upon arrival February 2 at Leyte they anchored in berth 234 San Pedro Bay, Dulag Leyte Philippines. At 2255 hours PT 488 and 489 [Motor torpedo boats] tied up astern. PT 489, skippered by Lt. W. B. Tatro USNR, had been part of Motor Torpedo Boat Squadron 33 under the command of Lt. Commander A. Murray Preston USNR. Lt. Comdr. Preston received the Medal of Honor from President Truman for "conspicuous gallantry and intrepidity" [Medal of Honor Citation] by taking PT 489 along with another, PT 363, into enemy fire to rescue a pilot Ens. Harold A. Thompson USNR of Fighter Squadron 26 after being shot down over Wasile Bay, Indonesia, 60 miles south of Morotai, September 16, 1944. Lt. Tatro and three others had Navy Crosses awarded. PT 489 was 80 ft. long and armed with a 40 mm gun, four 21 inch torpedo tubes and two .50 cal machine guns. PT boats had crews of around 15 to 17 men and could reach speeds of 41 knots.

They got underway on the 3rd and beached at Terraguna and then retracted. Later that day they hoisted anchor at 0645, to try to pull LST 769 off the beach, and succeeded. Unloading operations commenced on the 4th. After they discharged the army casuals and armored cars of the tank battalion, they then had to proceed down to Tacloban and put ashore the navy casuals. Some natives came alongside to trade and according to Weaver they tried to sell their own cigarettes to the natives. Dulag had been where some of the initial landings by General MacArthur's troops in the battle for the Philippines occurred. Indeed, some of the soldiers aboard had hit the beach in that same spot on the first day of the invasion. These soldiers had been back at Pearl in the hospital and now returning to their units. Japanese soldiers still fought on the island, but by that time they had fled inland or had been killed. One alert occurred there, but if there had been a raid it must have been far off. Neither did they see or hear any combat near them. The crew was impressed by having come so far without getting shot at or even seeing one Jap.

Duncan said of Leyte: "is quite lush, and the terrain is hilly. There are flats near the sea, but the land in that and the adjoining islands is pretty rough. The climate is apparently good. Rural dwellings are very grubby." (Adams, 2002)

At Dulag there had been a small village. A fairly large church wrecked by bombs stood in the middle of the village. The front wall stood intact, along with a cross at the peak. Some of the crew went ashore for an hour to have a look at the town. Riley recalled: "All the streets looked and smelled just like the pig pens that _____ kept back home. Just about ankle deep in mud and slime. There are few pavements on the main drag, but all the streets are lined with ditches which carry off sewage. You can smell it clear out to the ship." (Riley, 1943-1945) Houses had been merely shacks and the people wore rags, unless they acquired G.I. clothes. About eight light truck loads of American girls had been seen just off the transport. If they were nurses, then the crew could see the necessity of them being there. Riley, however, thought: "If they were WACS it is not only unnecessary, but a goddamn shame to send them into a place like this." (Riley, 1943-1945) As they went through the town one of them spotted a sign on city hall that said: "Notice- Do not pay more than two pesos for a marriage license." (Riley, 1943-1945) The ones that visited the town then headed back to the ship. When the crew members arrived back at the ship from the visit to Dulag, they could see natives peddling their wares all around the ship in their outriggers, trading grass hats, knives and just about anything for clothes, blankets etc. Money if offered had little value to the natives. On the 5th they had liberty to see a movie at 1900 hours. After the entertainment they went back to unloading and finished at 2400 hours. On the 6th they completed unloading the tank deck cargo and then lowered the truck ramp and began unloading main deck cargo. After unloading they tried to get the ship off the beach, but couldn't succeed until 1400 hours. Then back to Tacloban and an Army crane came alongside to port and unloaded the two LCVPs and two LCMs on the weather deck from around the LCT. Navy personnel disembarked after the boats. The skipper summed up Tacloban as: "a primitive, colorless, flaccid, squalid non sequitur. It's really a hole." (Adams, 2002) Finally they shoved off for Guadalcanal at 1300 hours on the 8th.

Leyte

Of all the places I have entered as either a liberator, conqueror, or camp-follower, Tacloban, Leyte, seemed to me the least desirable. It would be going pretty far to say it was dirtier than Porto Empedocle, a Sicilian town which I once located at night by the strong smell brought by an offshore breeze. And the people, while lacking in charm, do not have the sort of eyes which make you want to get back to the ship before sunset. There was mud, but there can be mud anywhere if it rains. I guess it's just that with all the vice and decadence of the South European countries and their African offshoots, they have some remaining vestiges of the great civilizations which once flourished there. And they have some of the strength that has made the European war such a hard and brutal one. Luzon may be different. Certainly in its day Manila must have been quite a city. But Tacloban is a primitive colorless flaccid squalid non sequitur. It's really a hole. Leyte is quite lush, and the terrain is hilly. There are flats near the sea, but the land in that and the adjoining islands is pretty rough. The climate is apparently good. Rural dwellings are very grubby.

February 9 the crew scrubbed the main deck in the afternoon. They sighted ten life jackets and several boxes floating close. A captain inspection preceded greasing the turnbuckles on the load deck on the 10th. At 0843 a breeches buoy was rigged to DE-704 [Destroyer Escort] and CPhM D. W. Bakes came aboard. At 0846 all lines of the breeches buoy were cast off and DE-704 resumed station. After his duties were done he was returned to DE-704 via breeches buoy again at 1318 hours. Most attended a basketball game on the tank deck at 1400 hours the next day.

The following day, the 12th of February, for those crew members who had not been shellbacks began the process of getting acquainted with the "Solemn Mysteries of the Deep", (Adams, 2002) or the initiation ceremony for crossing the equator. This has been a naval tradition for years, graduating pollywogs to shellbacks. Both officers and enlisted men participated. There had been only six men aboard who had crossed the equator before and therefore were shellbacks. The rest had to undergo the initiation ceremony. Shellbacks dressed as his Majesty King Neptune, his scribe Davy Jones and his Majesty's court. All the pollywogs, or wogs, had to appear before this court to answer for various "crimes" against King Neptune and his court. Punishment had to be then dealt out to the wogs. This consisted of having the head shaved clean in front of the ships company, a bedpan ceremony and a spanking. Often the ordeals would become increasingly embarrassing. The bedpan ceremony consisted of drinking some type of specially prepared elixir from the pan. On some ships the wogs would rebel and thus graduate to being a shellback. On others just by completing all the ordeals good naturedly they would graduate to shellbacks. The ceremony could also become rather tough, degrading and may involve beatings with fire hoses, which sent some to sickbay. All received very colorful 16 inch by 20 inch certificates signed by the captain. Max kept his as did Bob Weaver and others, some probably lost theirs or disposed of them. It usually named the sailor and the location that the ship crossed the equator. U.S.S. LST 791 crossed the equator at longitude 137 degrees 42 minutes east. This activity probably seemed childish, but it actually served a very important purpose, besides providing diversion in a dangerous theater of war, it actually help bond the crew together. It also ensured the old salts that their new shipmates could endure tough times at sea.

Crossing the Equator ceremony at Longitude 137 degrees 42 minutes east. J. A. Charbonnet is pictured as Davy Jones. (Adams, 2002)

Bedpan Ceremony (Adams, 2002)

Lt. Ralph Bohrer as Lookout for Davey Jones (Adams, 2002)

*Max's crossing the equator polywag to shellback
certificate. (Stripe-Bruhn, 2003-2010)*

The 14th of February saw their escort leave them and they started carrying running lights. So, the crew guessed there wasn't any Japanese in those waters, just flying fish. They sailed past the coast of New Guinea. General Quarters was sounded and firing practice was held. The skipper held inspection on the 17th and found the ship in good condition. On that day at 1720 hours they came across a water logged dingy which had been crudely converted into part of a raft. A couple of oars had been fixed upright and a makeshift sail was fashioned out of scraps of cloth made from a sugar sack and a pair of trousers squared rigged. Two large holes existed in the bottom of the boat and tiny fish could be found swimming around inside. Larger fish of many kinds could be seen hovering around with three, six to eight foot sharks also patrolling in the vicinity. No bodies or signs of bodies could be found or even evidence that people having been there recently.

They arrived at Guadalcanal at 1100 hours on the 19th and they beached in berth 12. The battle for Guadalcanal, Operation Watchtower, was fought between August 7, 1942 and February 9, 1943 and marked the transition from defensive to offensive operations by the allies. When the 791 arrived, Guadalcanal had been transformed into a major base for training, supply and staging of amphibious invasions in the western pacific.

Mail call sounded after four boxes of mail had been brought aboard. LST 762 couldn't get off the beach on the 20th. The 791 tried to pull 762 off the beech, but could not succeed. This had not been an unusual occurrence. Sometimes the crew of the ship would have to wait for the tide to come in and with or without help from another ship; they would get off the beach. Instances occurred when nothing could be done to get the ship off the beach, then the ship had to be salvaged, destroyed and abandoned. After the attempt they left the 762 to her future. Indeed, the LST 762 did get off the beach and also participated in the Okinawa invasion. She also saw service in Korea and Vietnam as the USS Floyd County. She finally was decommissioned April 1, 1975 and saw use as a commercial vessel until being scrapped in 1988. Seven LSTs had been lost during the war in all theaters due to grounding.

After ceasing efforts to tow LST 762 off the beach they proceeded to Hutchinson Creek, Florida Island and anchored there on 20th. On the 21st they moved to fueling depot and moored the port side to USS Ibex [fleet tanker] in Berth 24 Gavutu Harbor and commenced fueling. They returned to Hutchinson Creek and then proceeded to Tulagi, Ordnance Beech to begin loading operations. Tulagi was captured by the First Marine Raider Battalion on August 7, 1942 as part of Operation Watchtower. Later it was used as a base for a fleet of PT boats including President John F. Kennedy's PT 109 before becoming a base for supply.

The skipper, on the 21st, gave them a talk on the upcoming invasion that they would participate in. Loading operations started on the 22nd bringing aboard a bulldozer, 2 ½ ton truck, 500 rounds of white phosphorous mortar shells and 2500 rounds of high explosive mortar rounds, all stowed top side on the weather deck. Weaver remarked that had been crazy in how they had been tossing the mortar shells around. The crew worked through the night until 9 am the following day. Pay day also arrived for the previous two months. Weaver had small boat duty for the next two days.

Riley noted in his diary that they had been going through the chow line in the galley and one sailor looked at his tray, shook his head and said: "This chow is sure going to win the war, but how in the hell are we going to get the Japs to eat it." (Riley, 1943-1945) Riley's response had been that it really wasn't that bad. Food was generally plentiful if not gourmet. Max remembered eating a lot of spam and after the war he let his wife, Fern, know that he did not desire to see that dish again. The cooks usually kept treats available as well as a hot cup of coffee in the galley.

Richard Lundin, the ship's baker, a popular source of snacks. (Adams, 2002)

On the 24 they beached at berth 17 Kukum Beach, Guadalcanal and loaded 100 drums of 80 octane gas, 10 drums of diesel oil, 10 drums of SAE 50 oil, 2 drums of SAE 30 oil and 377 boxes of rations, stowed topside around and under the LCT. They spent the rest of the time cruising back and forth between Tulagi, Florida Island and Guadalcanal training for the coming invasion.

On the 27th they loaded 17 L.V.T.'s with their marine crews. L.V.T. or Landing Vehicle Tracked, also called an Alligator, had been a large tracked amphibious craft that could run off the end of the LST's ramp into the water and swim ashore. They then could roll up on the enemy beach like a tank. Each vehicle had four man crews and they could get 36 troops and/or supplies ashore under the cover of armor. The armament they carried included machine guns and some also had turreted cannons. Early models required the troops to climb in and out over the sides. Later models had a rear ramp that could be lowered to allow the troops to get in or out via back of the vehicle.

Causeway Platoon C-24 made up of twenty two Sea Bees under the command of Lt. N. E. MacDougal came aboard. The pontoons causeways responsibility fell to them. Two men of the 58th Sea Bees also came aboard. During the time in the Guadalcanal area the Sea Bees remodeled the bridge of the 791 with the Coast Guard emblem prominently painted on it. Also, on the 28th Lt. Ladd, Ens. O'Brian, and Comdr. Reith from LST Group 8 staff reported aboard to confer with the officers.

One of the L.V.T. crews had a little black and white mascot dog by name of Tojo. Some men described him as a cross between a dog and a hand grenade. Being a small dog he had been teased so badly that anybody who looked cross at him had a good barking and growl. The crew of L.C.T. 828 also had a mascot dog they called Duke. So LST 791 during one voyage had three dogs aboard. Other pets would find their way aboard from time to time and place to place.

LST 791 Bridge after remodeling by Seabees, note the Coast Guard Emblem. (Adams, 2002)

Lt. N. E. MacDougal Commander of Causeway Platoon C-24 (Adams, 2002)

On March 1st Lt. (jg) Amonette and Lt. (jg) Carnahan reported aboard for temporary duty. During the first part of March they practiced beaching and unloading the Marines in L.V.T.'s under combat conditions. During these episodes they would go to general quarters. On March 2nd Comdr. Reith, Lt. Ladd, Ens. O'Brian, SM1c Cutright, RM2c Williams, RM3c H. A. Jones, Y2c J. S. Jones and S1c De Frank of the Staff of LST Group 8 left the ship. On March 6 after the maneuvers they unloaded the L.V.T.'s on Guadalcanal. Lt. (jg) Amonette and Carnahan completed their temporary duties and left the ship. On the 7th they went to general quarters at 2200 hours as the ship next to them caught fire, but was controlled as they made preparations to retract. Weaver in the small boat brought a load of stores back to the ship on the 8th. The next day they went to Lalagos and brought some beer aboard. All day on the 8th and 9th they practiced beaching and retracting. On the 10th the L.V.T.'s came back aboard. On the 11th some of the L.V.Ts went ashore and came back with jeeps in them. Other cargo was loaded into the tank deck. This included in addition to the LVTs, a water distillation unit, 165 water drums, .50 cal ammunition, Marine field equipment, a Sea Bee welding unit and 1,048 half pound blocks of TNT. At 2000 hours they made an unsuccessful attempt to pull LST 951 off the beach. On the 12th they tried again and succeeded.

Guadalcanal

So much fighting, both naval and land, went on around Guadalcanal that you heard a lot about it. We went in there in August of 42, with light naval forces and too few Marines, but it was all we had. The Japanese navy was strong and plentiful. We avoided a decisive action, and the Japs, at the end of their extended supply lines, apparently did not feel like forcing one. But they sank plenty of our ships in that area, and by making the most of what we had we sank plenty of theirs. Because there are so many sunken ships in the area between Guadalcanal and Tulagi, it is called Iron Bottom Sound. Some of the pilots say there is a Jap carrier on the bottom there and that you can see planes sitting on her flight deck when the sea is smooth. But that may be just pilot's talk.

The islands along the sides of New Georgia Sound, now called the Slot, are the New Georgia Group, the Russells, Vella Lavella, Bouganville, Santa Isabel, and maybe other groups, though I believe they are the major ones. Of course there are more islands than I have drawn. At first we held only part of Guadalcanal. The Japs had the rest. They would send reinforcements down the Slot. There was much air and sub activity as well as surface engagements. Do you remember when three of our cruisers were lost there? They were at anchor near Guadalcanal. The Japs came in and apparently were undetected because of Savo Island, the little island out by itself. They came into the clear at point-blank range, it is said. The result is referred to by some as the battle of the sitting ducks.

You hear a lot about the steamy jungles of Guadalcanal. The rainfall there is the heaviest I ever saw. When it rains it rains hard then clears up for a while, but it isn't especially steamy aboard ship. Perhaps ashore it is. I was ashore very little. The vegetation is dense, the terrain rugged. It is bad fighting country. Japs have been cleaned out of most of the Solomons, but there are still some on Bougainville. The Australians are fighting them there. The Japs are reported by learned and distant commentators to be withering on the vine. According to the Australians "They take a bloody lot of withering."

The ship left Guadalcanal for Ulithi on the 12 of March in poor weather. General quarters had to be practiced every day, as did anti-aircraft gunnery practice. They would fire on a cloth sleeve target being towed by aircraft, the object being to hit the target and not the friendly towing aircraft. On the 16th Weaver put in for K.P. [Kitchen Police] and said it was good duty. LCS-712 [Landing Craft Support] came astern to take on fuel, water and bread. The crew received flash gear on the 17th. Flash gear was garments that crewmen wore to protect them from the flash and burn of guns. LCS-22 [Landing Craft Support] came alongside starboard and moored and Marvin Rowland F1c from Dexter Missouri was transferred for medical treatment. A rumor on the 19th going around had the ship going to condition 2 [Clear for Action]. First aid classes being held that day on the tank deck.

LST's during the war had pharmacist mates and sometimes doctors that took care of the medical needs of the crew. There had been three pharmacist mates on 791: Dilar Sanchez PhM3c from New York, James E. Morley PhM2c from Minnesota and Minott T. Wallace Jr. PhM1c. Later some surgeons and even a dentist came aboard the 791. These ships would sometimes act as minor hospital ships during beach landings. First aid and emergency procedures could be performed on the tank deck. When the ship was full of casualties they would transport the wounded to regular hospital ships. Thirty eight LSTs had been converted to hospital ships during the war and could be recognized by large white H's painted amidships on their hulls. LST hospital ships could not be afforded the Geneva Convention protection of being off limits to attack like regular all white painted hospital ships. A LST hospital ship could take care of 220 casualties on the tank deck and 150-175 in the troop quarters. They generally had four medical officers and 26 corpsmen. Another difference is that LST hospital ships had been armed and would carry supplies, tanks, pontoons, LCTs and invasion troops into battle. After the supplies and troops disembarked, the ships would then take up evacuation stations to receive the wounded. The pharmacist mates on combat LSTs generally knew the entire crew and it became their responsibility to make sure everyone, including the officers, was fit for duty. Marvin D. Rowland was sick and bunk ridden for three days and then on the 17th he was transferred to LCS-22 which had a doctor. It had been learned later that he had malaria.

They anchored in berth 206 northern anchorage at Ulithi on the 21st. The atoll of Ulithi, one of two advanced bases in the southwest Pacific had been used as a staging area for island invasions. Its lagoon, 22 miles long by 15 miles wide, is large enough to hold 700 ships, and indeed part of the Okinawa invasion force that formed up there had 617 ships. It had been seized by elements of the Army 81st Infantry Division on September 22, 1944 as part of the Palau Islands campaign. It is in the western Caroline

Islands 260 miles from Peleliu and was more than 1000 miles from the nearest Japanese base. The atoll is only 10 degrees north of the equator, making it detestably hot. Mog Mog island is one of 40 islets inside the lagoon and occupied an area of only 60 acres. It had various refreshment stands, a 500 seat chapel, and a 1200 seat theater. Bands would also frequent the island providing other entertainment. The facilities had been built to accommodate 8,000 enlisted men and 1,000 officers, but up to 15,000 servicemen would crowd little Mog Mog when the anchorage was full. Each serviceman was given coupons for two beers and separate areas had been established for officers. It would take in over 300 tons of supplies daily. It was known as the "grocery store of the Pacific." (Harper, 2001) Replenishment of supplies, fuel and ammunition became the purpose of this base. Floating dry docks provided repairs and upgrades to ships.

Duncan's commentary on the lagoons was: "The islands of the characteristic Central Pacific lagoons seem low, seldom raising more than a few feet above sea level. The unfortunate individuals who are stationed on these islands are also low. It is a monotonous existence. One may swim, or walk around the island and gather coconuts and seashells, or drink a few cool ones at the officers' club, but the facilities are not elaborate. There are usually movies, but in all my time overseas I have never seen but one good movie or heard of but one good one being shown. Most of them are old grade B or C movies. So much for lagoons. They are scrub islands with a hole in the middle." (Adams, 2002)

It was thought that Ulithi was safe from Japanese attack due to its distance from enemy bases. But the Japanese knew about the build up at Ulithi for the Okinawa invasion and mounted an operation called Tan No. 2 launching 24 twin engine Yokosuka P1Y "Frances" bombers on a suicide mission March 11, 1945. The operation was plagued by multiple problems including mechanical difficulties and bad weather. But one did make it to its target and crashed into the carrier [CV-15] USS Randolph's flight deck 15 feet from the stern at 2007 hours, killing 27.

On the 21st SC-712 [Sub Chaser] moored astern and took on fuel and water, which was completed after 3760 gallons of fuel oil and 1200 gallons of fresh water had been transferred. Then LCI 1069 [Landing Craft Infantry] moored astern and was pumped 6120 gallons of oil and 3800 gallons of fresh water. On the 22nd Pvt. W. A. Criscuolo suffered a deep cut of his forearm, cutting a vein. He was transferred to the USS Wayne [attack transport] for treatment. The officers and men of 2nd Battalion 22nd Marines came aboard on the 23rd. On the 24th they moored to the starboard side of AW-3, USS Pasig [a water distilling ship] at berth 229 and took on 16,054 gallons of fresh water. Then they moved to Berth 206 in the northern anchorage. 25th of the month saw her watering SC-712 and LCI-1069.

Ulithi Atoll 15, March 1945. American forces preparing for the invasion of Okinawa. Official U.S. Navy Photograph by Ensign Steinheimer (National Archives).

Weaver had been put back into the L.C.V.P. while at port. Weaver had duty for 15 hours on the 23rd in the boat, which became the duty boat for L.C.I. 1081, the flag ship of the amphibious ship group that 791 belonged to. L.C.I. or Landing craft Infantry a seagoing assault ship capable of landing on the beaches 200 troops by way of two gangways lowered to the beach had been developed at the same time as LSTs. Later production types had bow doors and ramp similar to LSTs. The cruising speed these craft could make amounted to 17 knots and they had been armed with antiaircraft guns, or modified to fire cannon or rockets. The duty boats function was to ferry the commander of the convoy or task force and carry messages between ships. At Ulithi the Marines and ancillary personnel came aboard from troop transports and they left harbor on the 25th at 1545 hours bound for Okinawa.

On the 26th the sea became rough from a small typhoon, requiring the crew to secure everything on the ship. LSTs being flat bottom ships don't take beam waves very well. So a storm plays havoc with these ships stability. Andrew Duncan said: "An LST will roll so jerkily that cargo has to be constantly tended to or it will drift." (Adams, 2002) On the 27 at 1547 hours LST 681 struck by an unusually heavy wave had its pontoon barge #40 lost overboard. LST 769, under command of Lt. Bertini positioned head of them in column, also had pontoons causeways hauled on its sides. On the 29th he pulled out hard and dropped back between columns. The starboard column saw what happened and opened up to allow him out into the sea and minimize his roll. But it became futile. He lost a pontoon causeway as did several other ships. At about sunset the 769 got back on station. Other deck board items started parting securing chains on other ships and crashing about, such as cranes, bulldozers, trucks etc. On several occasions the convoy changed course in order to reduce the rolling of the ships and prevent the pontoons from being pounded and hopefully reducing the risk of losing any more.

Only a few of the ships had their pontoons as long as the 791. Metal fatigue had set in to the securing gear. Early in the morning 28 of March, 0200 hours, a sharp crash sounded as a clamp securing the aft end of one of the pontoon causeway was carried away in the storm. This caused that aft end to be "hopping around with each roll as though it was ready to continue the voyage alone." (Adams, 2002) No spare securing gear had been available on board. Permission from the convoy commander had to be obtained to repair and secure the pontoon. The skipper then told MacDougall to break out his welding gear. They decided to cut into parts of the ship that had been nonessential if necessary to keep the pontoons. With the help of the sea bees and acetylene torches the pontoon was secured to the ship by welding braces fashioned from other parts to the hull. This took couple of hours and fortunately had been accomplished without being spotted due to heavy cloud cover. The storm made the sea rough for several days. Weaver had done K.P. since they left Ulithi and he felt ill, but denied it was from the rough seas. The storm meant enemy planes couldn't find them. Submarines also had difficulty scouting and setting up for torpedo shots in rough seas. So in a way the typhoon in one sense made the convoy safer.

The Perils Of The Sea (As The Marine Insurance Policies Pot It)

In default of mail I shall chronicle a few heavy weather incidents which sound kind of dull but had their moments. How much the public is told about the details of carrying pontoon causeways is an indeterminate which will make me a little vague. But I suppose the numerous articles about them have informed you that they weigh 90 to 100 tons, cost the government $200,800 apiece, and are of a size that is quite in keeping with their cost and weight. Well, we lugged a couple of these cozy little items a good many thousand miles, but they and the weather didn't really get cantankerous until we stood out of Ulithi for Okinawa. It had been messy before, but not too bad. The main thing *an LST hates is a beam sea. She rolls so jerkily that cargo has to be constantly tended or it will come adrift. (LST's have an 8\ second roll.) We put out of Ulithi on 25 March into a nasty patch of weather and it was as bad or worse until the 31st, when it providentially broke. (That, by the way, is the third time in four invasions that the weather has turned good just before we went in.) It seemed there was a good chance that the beam sea we had on the 25th would hold, and it certainly did. we couldn't deviate far enough from our base course to get much relief.*

Only a few of the ships had their pontoons as long as we, which was a good thing because metal fatigue was setting in on the securing gear. Every now and then a big sea would kick us hard and something new would break. We had a detachment of Seabees aboard whose contributions to the invasion was the care and feeding of our pontoons. They knew their job, like most Seabees, and when something carried away they were right on the scene to weld it together again. That system worked all right when only one thing came apart at a time, but sometimes more than one came apart and then we had to cross our fingers pretty fervently. Every now and then something would go overboard or be broken irreparably, and we were steadily losing ground. None of us had been able to get any spare securing gear, I guess because of the size of the operation. McDougall, the Seabee officer, and I had talked about this and had decided that we would cut into parts of the ship that were nonessential if necessary but that we were going to keep the pontoons. The 769 was next ahead of us and I was concerned about him. They had operated under my command at a time when I had taken four other LST's on a little junket. We had been together for couple of months and I suspected his situation was close. Bertini* (see page 39), the captain, was a good sailor, but I was afraid his pontoon might go in the drink some dark night right in my way. It must have been about the 29th, in the afternoon that he pulled out hard and dropped back between the columns. The starboard columns saw what was happening and opened up to let him go out into the sea and minimize the roll, but it was no use. We couldn't see it too well for the rain and mist, but we got the general

51

idea. No one was hurt or lost overboard, though. more was lost that day by another ship and one the next day. Poor Bertini got back in station about sunset and about ten that night turned on his breakdown lights and hauled out again. This time it was a crane, which had parted its securing chains and was charging about like Victor Hugo's cannon. To make it worse, it had ripped into some oil drums and there was no decent footing. Much to their credit, they were able to get it secured again. I heard his report on the radio and we certainly felt for him. About 0200 there was a sharp crash and we began to fee for ourselves. Several securing members had carried away simultaneously and the after end of the pontoon causeway was hopping around with each roll as though it was ready to continue the voyage alone. I told MacDougall to break out his welding gear and charged back up to the conn. The convoy commodore gave us permission to weld so the Japs, if they were looking, were treated to the weird spectacle of an LST wallowing around drunkenly and emitting about as much blue light as the Brooklyn Navy Yard. We welded and cut for a couple of hours and were very relieved when at the end of it the causeway seemed firmly with us once more. Essentially, we had simply welded the pontoon to the side of the ship, since most of the securing gear was gone.

31 July 1945

The next day we continued to embellish a structure which is peculiar enough as originally designed. The weather continued to remind us of the North Atlantic and there was a fairly deep kicking sea. There were low traveling grey clouds with occasional rain, and you know how slatey the water gets in that weather for subs. But at least planes couldn't find us and it was rough. On D-1 the wind and sea died down, the sun shone, and life was good again. As usual, the fine weather raised our spirits greatly, and if anyone had seemed interested we would have been glad to carry the pontoons on to Tokyo. I can see that I should have told you more about anyone I enjoy as much as Bertini. He is a little Italian, 32, and had his own 125-foot patrol boat out of San Pedro for a while. Those who have operated on small boats always have a feeling for their ships that big-ship men lack. When we meet we always spend a lot of time talking about our ships. Bertini always starts off pessimistically. He waves his hands, shrugs his shoulders, screws up his little dark face. Things are very bad. "And then guess what happened..." he will say. commencing a still more trying incident in the existence of the 769. "You wouldn't believe it" usually ushers in some tale which sounds as though it could only end in the loss of the ship with all hands. About this time somebody usually clubs him on the back and says "Where did she go down, Bert?" So he grins wryly and says come out pretty well, all things considered.

The Seabees are very fine. I think they are the most competent workmen I have seen during the war. They are renowned. for their ingenuity and are very industrious. They are masters at handling heavy weights. MacDougall and his crowd stayed at Okinawa about six weeks, then were relieved.

On the 31st they come to within 50 miles of the target on their starboard bow. At 0835 hours a flight of Hellcats had been spotted off the starboard bow. 1035 hours a TBF Avenger was sighted off the port quarter. A B-24 Liberator could be seen off the port beam. At 1750 hours a flight of F4F Hellcats had been spotted just off the port quarter. A large steamer fully lighted had been observed and tracked by the crew on the port beam at about 15 miles steaming in a southerly direction and could not be identified. LCI-705 came alongside to the port quarter and transferred mail. The wind and sea had died down and the sun shone all day. Riley described the ship as crowded. With her usual compliment of officers and men, the Marines on board with landing craft crews and the Sea Bees a total of 532 souls were aboard. The skipper described it as "troops were all over the ship like ants on a piece of fruitcake." (Adams, 2002) Many of the marines had slept topside under the L.C.T. due to the humidity and heat in the troop quarters. Before the invasion Max remembered that the marines had been given steak dinners and fresh water showers. He knew that the battle was going to be tough for them. The skipper ordered condition 2 [clear for action] to be set.

OKINAWA INVASION

Operation Iceberg was going to be the last great amphibious invasion and battle of World War Two in the Pacific Theater of operations, but the men of LST 791 didn't know that. Okinawa is largest island in the Ryukyus chain at 66 miles long by 19 miles at its widest and with an area of 485 square miles. Being only 340 miles from the main islands of Japan it made the ideal jumping off base for the future invasion of the home islands. At the beginning of the operation the U.S. Army began with 102,250 soldiers. The Marine Corps began operations with 88,500 troops. Those numbers alone make it the largest amphibious invasion in history, including the Normandy D-Day invasion. Indeed the Okinawa invasion had the largest number of LSTs ever assembled for the initial landings, 343 LSTs. The Marine and Army Divisions made up the 10th Army under command of Lieutenant General Simon Bolivar Buckner. Over 1300 ships composed the allied invasion armada. Ships of every type from fleet carriers, battleships, cruisers, destroyers, attack transports, cargo ships to LST's, LCI's and other landing craft of every description participated.

Task Force 51, the Joint Expeditionary Force, composed of five smaller task forces and three task groups under Vice-Admiral Richmond K. Turner, the Commander of Pacific Amphibious Forces. LST 791 was part of the Northern Attack Force (TF 53) commanded by Rear-Admiral Lawrence F. Reifsnider. It had two transport groups, each with over 20 attack transports and attack cargo transports. It also had 67 LSTs transporting amphibious tractors and pontoon causeways plus screening destroyers. LST 791 was part of Green Unit under the command of Commander George Reith USNR consisted of the following LSTs along with the 791: 1013 [the flagship], 951[H], 952 [H], 627, 483, and 681. LSMs [Landing Ship Medium] 270, 271, 274 also made up part of that command. LSMs being smaller sea going vessels could only land 5 Sherman tanks or 54 troops. In overall command of the invasion was the legendary Admiral Raymond A. Spruance, the commander of the Fifth Fleet and Central Pacific Forces.

Okinawa   1 May 1945

Okinawa may not be the Pearl of the Pacific, but it looks more desirable from a military standpoint than most of the places I've seen out here. It has a bunch of airfields, some good anchorages, and, of all things on Pacific Islands, a little harbor. At this writing Naha, the harbor, is still in the hands of the Japs. But it is just a matter of time before it falls. When we start bombers working from Okinawa the Japanese home folks are going to have their problems. Of course Okinawa will be bombed too off and on but we'll probably hurt them worse than they hurt us.

On the way up to O. The weather was rough, rainy, and miserable. Troops were all over the ship like ants on a piece of fruitcake. We were able to feed them well, and most of them ate, but it was a pretty hard life for them. We ran from Ulithi right in the trough of the sea the 1200 miles to Okinawa. But a couple of days from O. The weather broke and we had good steaming. D-day (L-day as it was called in this operation for no reason I know of) was a beautiful calm cloudless day. The night before we steamed under a beautiful moon, which the Japs appreciated more than we did. Their attacks were light and comparatively ineffective.

Our rehearsal for this operation had been excellent, and on the morning of D-day we all did our stuff as planned.

The supporting naval bombardment far exceeded our fondest hopes and was quite the heaviest I have ever seen. However, the fact that there was no counter-fire was a great surprise to me. The landings were almost entirely unopposed. The stories of the ease which the beach and adjacent areas were secured are quite true. Apparently the Japs committed their entire force to a defense elsewhere, and did not man their positions where our people went in.

And they did have excellent prepared positions from which a small number of men could have fought effectively enough to have slowed our advance and made the securing of the beachhead costly.

The Japs expended a great many planes in action against our naval forces, and in attacks on our ground troops, but their expenditures are so out of proportion to their results that I do not think their air power can do anything but decline as the unequal struggle goes on. They are losing far more planes than we. Many of their planes are intercepted on the way to the place where they are going to do their bombing. It seems to me from the reports of specific engagements with which I am familiar that at least half of the Jap planes must be shot down before they get where they're going. By the time they have run the gauntlet the rest of the Japs are disorganized and scattered, so that they are unable to launch a coordinated attack. Of course it isn't always like that, but I have never heard of any big air group getting past our fighter cover – maybe 3 or 4 at a time but no more. Once they do get in, the various weapons now carried by naval ships knock most of them down. Some are successful, but they certainly pay for their successes. The Germans got better results at less cost. We were all pleased when the Yamato was sunk. She was supposedly a very fine battleship.

The Japs have very little naval strength left. By the way, the fine weather *of D-day degenerated about D plus 3, but by that time we had our people pretty well set up ashore. The operation seemed to run off pretty well on the whole. It was organized intelligently and considering its magnitude the details of execution were adequately handled. There was a thorough rehearsal which readied us for the mechanics of the operation and familiarized us with the basic problems involved. It was the easiest invasion I have ever been in and if we can arrange for them to all be like this I will have few harsh words for the Pacific theater.*

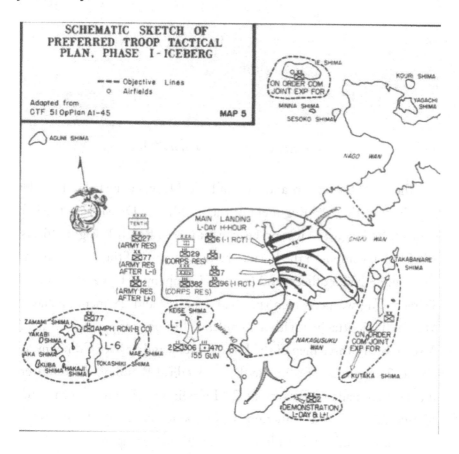

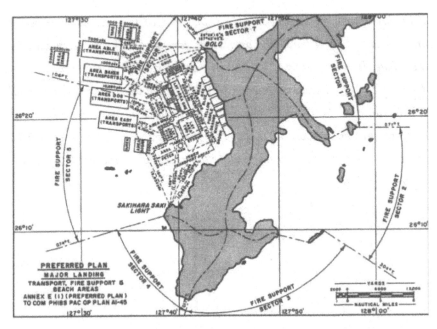

Okinawa invasion plans. (National Archives)

The job of the officers and crew of LST 791 was to be to land the 2nd Battalion, of the 22nd Regiment of the 6th Marine Division on the left flank of the Hagushi invasion beaches at Green Beach 1. Eight officers and 87 men composed the Headquarter Company of the 2nd Battalion. Company F had 3 officers and 66 men. Company G had 2 officers and 57 men. The weapons company had 1 officer and 28 men. A Naval Medical Unit attached with a complement of one officer and 11 men. Also on board three men of the Headquarters and Service Company as well as 2 corpsmen of company B, 6th Medical Battalion. One officer and 11 men made up Battery D, 2nd Battalion, 15th Marines of the 6th Marine Division, who functioned as forward observers. Two officers and eight men of the Sixth Joint Assault Signal Company would go in with 2nd Battalion 22nd Marine Regiment. The Second Section of the 3rd Bomb Disposal Platoon of the 1st Bomb Disposal Company had also been on board and included 1 officer and 4 men. In addition there was

Company A and B of 4th Amphibian Tractor Battalion, Fleet Marines which included three officers and 65 men who operated the LVTs.

The 6th Marine Division under the command of Major General Lemuel Shepherd along with 1st and 2nd Marine Divisions made up the Third Amphibious Corps commanded by Major General Roy Geiger. General Geiger had to be somewhat of an anomaly; after General Buckner had been killed by Jap artillery shrapnel June 18 on Okinawa, he became the only Marine General and aviator to command an operational field army during the war. Albeit, it was for a short few days until Army General [Vinegar] Joe Stillwell assumed command. The 22nd Marine regiment had fought on Eniwetok, Guam and the Marshall islands. The 2nd Battalion of the 22nd Marines had the privilege of being commanded by Lt. Col. Horatio Woodhouse Jr. Lt. Adams got to know Col. Woodhouse well from wardroom conversations and described him as "wonderful gentleman and a fine officer." (Adams, 2002) A physically small slender man, but very intelligent and had been described as a fine tactician. (Hallas, 1996) "He also happened to be a cousin of General Shephard." (Hallas, 1996) He assumed command of the battalion on Guam.

Lt. Col. Horatio C. Woodhouse(UNMC National Archive)

In spite of his anticipation of a tough invasion, the colonel drafted a letter that had to be given to the crew of LST 791 on a later date, it read:

United States Marine Corps
Easter Sunday
1 April, 1945.
To the Officers and men of LST 791:

On behalf of the Marines whom you have safely brought to their target and whom you have had crowded on your ship these last seven days. I'd like to thank you all for being such wonderful host to us.

It has been indeed a pleasure to have traveled with you, and to have known you all. Your cooperation has been outstanding and we wish to thank you for all you have done to make our stay with you enjoyable.

Best of luck to you all- Happy Easter Bunny.
H. C. Woodhouse Jr.
Lt. Col. USMC

The first day of the invasion of Okinawa came to be called L-Day, Landing Day or Love Day. Riley noted that ever since L minus 1 they had been standing general quarters continuously, with the gun crews and repair parties sleeping at their stations. Stripe and Thornhill with five other crewmen manned the forward twin 40 mm mount. Riley's station had been in the Conn, conning tower or bridge, where enemy planes could be tracked there fairly easily from bogey reports that came in over the radio. Several groups of ships could be seen within the horizon of 791. Astern of the 791 some transports came under attack. Tracers could be seen. Increase in air attacks could be expected at dawn and sunset. This is because for a brief time aircraft can see the ships clearly, but it was difficult for the ships to see the planes. Sometimes firing would be seen or heard and then a short bright glow from a plane that crashed. Rarely, a bright glow from a ship on fire could be observed. Riley couldn't stay awake for 24 hours, so he had to be relieved for a couple hours by a "fellow whose station didn't have to be manned until action occurred." (Riley, 1943-1945) Sometime later someone shook Riley waking him and told him that his presence became necessary in the Conn. When he got up there it was all over. An escort ship shot down a Jap plane identified as a Zeke [Zero] at 0215 hours, but they didn't get a chance to shoot at anything. First spotted about 1500 yards out at a height of 100 feet and flew over the convoy. Riley recorded that they entered the East China Sea the night before L-Day passing south of Okinawa and continued toward China and then doubled back toward the invasion beaches. Just before sunup on April 1 they had been a little north of Cape Zampa Misaki heading toward the invasion beaches.

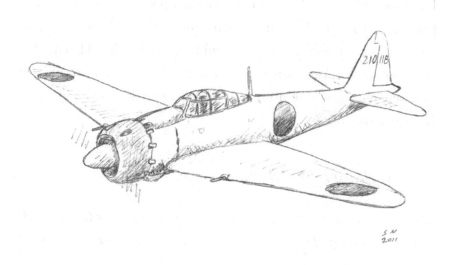

Japanese Zero or Mitsubishi A6M (Scott Nelson 2011)

The invasion had been preceded by a shore bombardment from 16 inch naval rifles to 20 mm anti aircraft guns for six days. This had been a response by the Navy to criticism by the Marines that there had been only three days of bombardment prior to landings at Iwo Jima. An umbrella of allied aircraft participated in bombing, strafing and rocketing the eight mile length of beach landing zones. Prior to H-hour 44,825 rounds of 5 inch to 16 inch shells, 33,000 rockets and 22,500 mortar shells had been fired from the fleet.

At 0530 hours all ships reported being at Condition 1[battle stations] on approach to the landing area, course 159 degrees true and speed of 7 knots in formation. At 0605 hours a small float plane appeared swooping down as if to attack and straightened out on course between the line of bombardment ships and the line of LST's, LSM's, and LCI's that had fanned out for the invasion. Everybody within range began shooting at him. Accuracy not being very good; it was the volume of fire that proved effective enough to do the work. He burst into flames and crossed the forward port ships in the convoy and crashed a little ahead and to starboard of the lead ship. Everyone started cheering wildly. The public address system then blared: "You have just seen an American plane shot down. Now you understand why you were not allowed to fire." (Riley, 1943-1945) The crew and troops just stood dazed.

How We Accounted For A Plane.   Sept. 7 1945

There was general air activity the night before the landings on Okinawa. We could keep fairly good track of the planes by the bogey reports that came in. There were several groups of ships within our horizon. Sometimes there was firing, sometimes the short bright glow which means a plane has crashed, more rarely there was the sustained flame or a ship on fire. The one attack on our own convoy was unsuccessful, but alerted the ship's company to the full possibilities of the situation.

An increase in aerial attacks is normally expected at dawn and sunset. For a short time the planes can see ships very- clearly and it is most difficult to see the planes.

Just before the sun came up we were a little north of Cape Lampa Misaki, standing down toward the area where we would launch our LVT's. There was a lovely pink eastern sky, and our lovely battleships were ranged in their bombardment line ready to commence their work.

Astern of us some transports were under attack. A plane went down. Some more tracer began to arc up from a point below the horizon and swing deliberately across the sky, following a plane. A small float plane appeared on the port side of our convoy. He was going the same way we were. When he was just abeam of the center ships two of them opened up. Nearly all the others followed suit. Accuracy was not exceptional, but there was enough volume to do the work. The plane's right wing went down with the gesture which seems almost animately to say "I'm done for." He burst into flames, crossed the forward port ships in the convoy, and crashed a little ahead and to starboard of the leading ship in our column. when he began to flame our troops and ships' company cheered wildly, and the cheering rose to a crescendo when he crashed harmlessly. They were almost dazed at our public-address system announcement "You have just seen an American plane shot down. Now you understand why you were not allowed to fire.

0631 hours the formation executed speed 1 or slowing down. 0637 hours they turned to approach the LST area. At 0646 hours ships on the left flank closed in to 300 yards and 0649 hours at prearranged signal drop anchors. All Green Unit ships became anchored 5,500 yards off green beach 1 and 2. Far left flank and closest to beach was LST 627 and 250 yards to starboard of her was LST 483. Every 250 yards starboard was another landing ship and in order were LSM 271, LST 952[H], LST 951[H] the Red Unit LST 712, Red Unit LST 833 and then Green Unit LST 681. Behind the far port or left flank anchored 300 yards astern was the 791, then 250 yards to starboard LSM 274, another 250 yards to starboard LST 1013 and finally to starboard of her LSM 270 of Green Unit. By 0656 hours all ships of Green unit reported ready to launch wave guide boats and proceed.

April 1, 1945, April fool's Day, Easter Sunday, L-Day saw LST 791 anchored off shore in 28 fathoms of water and 600 feet of cable on the stern anchor out with the weather clear. At 0711 hours, the debarking of 5th and 7th invasion waves would commence. The Marines of the 2nd Battalion 22nd Marine Regiment waited with great anxiety and anticipation in the LVTs with engines running. In the closed space of the tank deck engine exhaust had to be actively vented to the outside via 12 fan vented 40 inch diameter 8 foot high exhaust stacks and fresh air taken in. The ventilation system noise added to the cacophony of the tank deck. Since this outfit had veterans of other island invasions, they knew what to expect. LVT's lined up two abreast one behind the other. Bow doors then opened and the ramp lowered. Upon the famous words being spoken by the invasion commander, Admiral Kelly Turner, and relayed to the ships, "Land the landing force". The crewman, in the traffic control station that monitored vehicle traffic and operated a traffic light system, would then indicate when the LVT drivers should begin to disembark. LVTs with the clanking of their treads on the steel deck adding to the noise would then drive off the ramp one by one into the surf and head for the beach. After the LVTs landed their troops ashore, they would then return for more. At 0828 hours debarkation had been completed with the launching of the 10th wave, which came by LCVPs from the transports to the LSTs to be disembarked in reserve LVTs. The marine objective in front of Green beach that day had been Yontan airfield.

*The Invasion Beach at Okinawa, First Objective
Yontan Air Field (National Archives)*

After the troops had disembarked the two hospital LSTs, 951(H) and 952(H), then ordered to proceed to evacuation stations. LSMs had also been ordered to proceed on to duties assigned to various transports.

Weaver being in the LCVP at 0830 hours about 200 yards from shore, admitted that he felt pretty nervous. With utter amazement that day he didn't even see a Jap or heard a bullet. Lt. Duncan remarked later: "the fact that there was no counter-fire was a great surprise to me. The landings were almost entirely unopposed." (Adams, 2002) That night Weaver stood watch in the small boat 50 feet from shore.

Within the first hour of invasion over 16,000 troops came ashore. With the beach head secure other combat troops came ashore, followed by tanks via landing craft, LSMs and floatation devices. After them, the ammunition and other supplies began arriving. By the end of the day the invasion beachheads of eight miles wide by three to four miles deep had become well secured and with the two primary objectives that day of the airfields being captured. By nightfall that day 60,000 troops had been put ashore. Total cost for that day was 28 killed, 104 wounded and 27 missing. The trap the Japanese planned had not been on the beaches, but in the southern part of the island.

LVT heading into the beaches on April 1, 1945,
L-Day from LST 791. (Morley, 2003-2005)

Invasion. Marines loading onto Higgins boat during beach
landings, as seen from bow. (Morley, 2003-2005)

MEDAL OF HONOR
WINNER ON BOARD

Of those marines that disembarked that day they included a 19 year old corporal James L. Day. May 14, Day and his unit had been ordered to try and hold the western slope of Sugar Loaf Hill. That hill anchored the western end of the infamous Shuri Line, the main Japanese defensive line in the south of Okinawa. The name of Sugar Loaf Hill had been christened to that infamous piece of real estate by Lt. Col. Woodhouse himself, a name he would use for objectives on training exercises at Guadalcanal. That hill stood only 50 feet high by 300 yards long, but had been festooned with tunnels and defensive positions. Day and his unit made it up the hillside through heavy artillery fire and stumbled into a 30 foot shell crater. Almost instantly more than 20 Japanese soldiers attacked them. As his squad rose to defend their position they had been hit by bullets and shell fragments. After a furious fire fight the attack had been beaten back. Three of Day's comrades lay dead, three wounded and another Pfc. Bertoli lay writhing in pain from dengue fever. As Sgt. Narolian West and two stretcher bearers arrived into the crater the Japanese launched another attack. Day reacted swiftly spinning around and immediately shooting three enemy soldiers. During this fight two of the wounded Marines had been killed. West begged Day to go back with them, as did Bertoli and a wounded replacement named McDonald, but he refused. Night fell and enemy soldiers crept up the slopes as flares lit up the battlefield. Day waited until he could hear them and then threw hand grenades at the shadows. (McConnell, 1998)

With day light the slope around the crater had been shelled with mortars. Then enemy troops surged up after the barrage lifted. Day rose and fought back. This outpost ahead of the allied lines was critical. By holding off the enemy Day gave the Marines time to find a way to push through and the Japanese knew it. They had to drive him off Sugar Loaf. By late afternoon of the 15th, Day and McDonald at the edge of the crater, fired bursts into the Japanese down the slopes. A Jap anti tank gun fired and killed McDonald instantly and shrapnel cut Day's hands. Day dragged a machine gun to the edge of the crater and fired until the enemy retreated. That night U.S. phosphorous mortar shells burst around the crater. Some white phosphorous fragments hit Bertoli. Day smothered the phosphorous on Bertoli's neck and arms with mud. Day then felt a stabbing, burning pain in his right foot as a chunk of phosphorous burned through his shoe. He covered it with mud. (McConnell, 1998)

At dawn on the 16th, Day heard boots in the mist and reacted quickly by shooting at shadows in the mist only 40 feet away. All day long there occurred bursts of terror and noise interspersed with ringing silence. At nightfall struggling to stay awake, Day fired at and took out two enemy machine gun crews. Morning came and a Marine lieutenant suddenly appeared in the crater and ordered Day to pull back. An American battalion had now been advancing their way. Day and Bertoli staggered down the slope through the column of Americans. The battalion found more than 70 dead Japanese soldiers around that position with 56 in front of shell crater itself. Day's three days and three nights on Sugar Loaf proved to be the key to smashing the Shuri line. Lt. Col. Woodhouse then ordered witness statements to be taken from the survivors in order to recommend him for the Medal of Honor. Seven statements collected and a citation had been drafted. (McConnell, 1998)

Lt. Col. Woodhouse was shot by a sniper in the head and killed on the 30th of May near Naha the Capital. Dale Bertoli had been shot in the back of the neck on June 8 and died aboard the USS Relief on the 12th. Day's company commander, Owen Stebbins, had been wounded on May 12 by machine gun fire to the legs and evacuated, this occurred just two days prior to Day's heroic action. Years later, Stebbins heard about the action and doggedly pursued the medal for Day. Stebbins died in 1996. The nephew of the company commander found a box of Day's records and continued the effort for his uncle to get Jim Day recognized. Finally, on January 20th, 1998 Major General James Day [ret.] stood in the East Room of the White House and received the Medal of Honor from then President Clinton. The Medal of Honor recommendation never moved up the chain of command after Okinawa. Day not only survived, he also served honorably in Korea and Vietnam. Day retired from the Marines a Major General. At the end of the Okinawa battle Marine losses had been counted at 2,938 dead or missing with 13,708 wounded. Army dead and missing counted 4,625 with 18,099 wounded. Only 13 men of the 343 Marines and Navy Corpsmen transported by LST 791 survived the battle of Okinawa.

Sugar Loaf Hill Okinawa (USMC/National Archives)

Gen. Day with his Marine comrades 1998: (Adams, 2002)
Left to Right: Charles E. Stines, Raymond Schindler, General James
L. Day, George Niland, James Chaisson, and Lenly M. Cotton.

SHIP OPERATIONS AND KAMIKAZE ATTACKS

On the 2nd of April the 791 had been underway and at 0530 hours went to general quarters. Anti-aircraft fire could be seen 3 miles away. At 0726 hours she anchored off shore in 33 fathoms with 325 feet of stern anchor cable played out. While there, they commenced with launching the port pontoon causeway at 0746 hours and the starboard pontoon causeway at 0827 hours. Launching the causeways would be accomplished by simply releasing the securing gear, letting them fall into the water and drift away from the ship by inertia. By 1200 hours the causeways had been towed away from the ship. Lt. N. E. MacDougal, CEC, USNR and his Seabees departed the ship shortly thereafter. The Seabees stayed on Okinawa for 6 weeks before being relieved. The deployment of the many pontoon causeways from the reefs to the solid ground of the beaches eased the problem of moving supplies from ship to shore. Landing craft could tie up and transfer their cargo directly into trucks. Red Beach one, with Yontan field inland from it had the longest causeway of 1,428 feet.

"Two of the great weapons of this war are the pontoon and the bulldozer" commented Lt. Duncan in correspondence to his uncle. (Adams, 2002) The Hagushi beaches are not the best to beach a LST or other ships, therefore requiring the pontoon causeways. Coral reef could extend 400 to 500 yards out from shore. On the reef there would be 0-7 feet of water at low tide. With dump trucks and bulldozers they would push fill out along the highest portion of the reef, using oil drums filled with dirt to shore up the sides. On top of this they would improvise a road. The road would have to be repaired from time to time due to erosion from the sea, but not too fast due to the reef breaking up the high seas. Pontoon causeways would be floated into place to meet the road at high tide and anchored. Pontoons would be partially or fully flooded to provide stability, depending on the depth of the reef. Inshore pontoon was always completely flooded. Seaside out shore pontoon was not flooded and free to move at high tide. Chains were used to secure it to the middle pontoon.

Later during the invasion on May 22 the 791 was ordered to unload and they moored the bow to the end pontoon of a causeway. The ship had 500 feet of stern anchor cable out and two lines to the seaward pontoon. Also, they chained the bow ramp to the causeway; because the appliance designed to hold the ship steady had been torn off by a previous ship. On the second day of unloading a strong south-southwest wind and rough sea came up. They put two more chains on the bow ramp and doubled the lines. As insurance they put a LCVP boat on the port side to push and hold the 791 steady. The cargo of ammunition was badly needed. As the seas and wind increased, under normal conditions the unloading operation would have been postponed. The skipper asked for permission to "take any steps that might become necessary." (Adams, 2002) About midnight the skipper had been at the bow watching the docking shudder and shake with each wave. A message came in that a cold front with high winds was expected. The boat had to be ordered to stop pushing when the cold front hit and initial gust reversed the swing of the ship and snapped the ramp from the pontoon chains before the boat could check the swing. The ship had snapped the ramp to pontoon chains carrying away pieces of the second pontoon. Except for one or two chains the outboard pontoon was free of the middle one. As a very heavy rain began they closed the bow, hauled up the stern anchor and cast off from the pontoon, using the boat to hold the course steady and when clear they dropped the bow anchor to ride out the storm. Seabees got to work restoring the causeway to resume unloading operations as soon as the weather calmed. By dawn they reestablished the connection with the causeway and proceeded with unloading.

Engineer's Items

Some of the large ammunition ships which carried the stuff up to Okinawa originally had unsuccessful encounters with the Kamikaze, so some LST's were thrown in as pinch-hitters. We were among those lucky enough to be nominated, and picked up 1183 tons of plain and fancy explosives at Guam. We also got 38 tons of mail. Returning to Saipan, we took a small tug in tow (they threw it in for nothing) and set out. There were two other LST's and a few harebrained escorts.

Contrary to what may be the popular view, ammunition is good cargo. They always stow it well so that it does not shift, it is clean, and it furnishes none of the small incidental problems that vehicles or general cargo present. Also, when you carry ammunition you don't carry personnel. Carrying personnel is our job, but when we legitimately get out of it we don't mind. Another thing is that ammunition is good and heavy and sets the hull well down in the water, making the ship ride well. We had carried ammo from Mobile to Pearl and were familiar with it.

However, people who do not believe in predestination are apt to feel that such cargo causes a temporary alteration of one's life expectancy, and sometimes other ships have a tendency to avoid you if you have the red flag flying. One's normal care in handling the ship is increased by the inadvisability of bumping anything very hard. Most ammo is fairly inert, but in a mixed ammo cargo there is so much fused stuff that accidents are possible. Since you (my uncle) are accustomed to the handling of explosives, I thought you might be interested in the foregoing. It also gives a little background to an accident which took place while we were unloading. Two of the great weapons of this war are the pontoon and the bulldozer, and I often wish you could see them as they are used-in the forward areas. The beaches at hagushi were not the best in the world and it was necessary to use pontoon causeways for handling major loads in quantity. Here is how they do it. The coral reef extends out some distance, say about 400 or 500 yards. On the reef there is about zero to 7 feet of water, depending on the state of the tide and the indentations on the reef. In many places the reef was above water at low tide. With dump trucks and bulldozers they push a fill out along the highest convenient portion of the reef, using oil drums filled with dirt to bulwark the sides. The top of this made road is above high tide. Though the road has to be repaired from time-to time i t does not usually erode too fast because the reef breaks up the big seas, when there are any. However, as the road goes out it meets stronger opposition from the sea, and ultimately it is necessary to use pontoon causeways. These are floated into place at high tide and anchored, sometimes after preparatory demolition work on the reef. Pontoon sections may be wholly or partially flooded for stability, depending on the depth of the reef. The inshore one in the diagram was completely flooded, I believe, and the middle one was partially or completely flooded. They were good and stable. However, the seaward pontoon was free to move at high tide, and though grounded at the inshore end had play. It was chained to the middle pontoon by a good many chains.

We were ordered in there one night to unload. We beached, or rather moored our bow to the pontoon. We had 500 feet of stern anchor cable out and had lines to the two seaward pontoons. In addition, we had chained the bow ramp to the seaward causeway because an appliance designed to hold it steady had been torn off by a previous customer. On the second day of the unloading a strong wind and sea came up from about south southwest. We put two more chains on the bow ramp, doubled our lines, and finally put a boat on the port side to push and thus help hold her still.

The ammunition was badly needed, but the wind and sea increased so that under normal conditions we would have called it off. However I asked for discretion to take any steps which might become necessary, and upon getting it, including permission to secure unloading, if desired, felt fortified. Just about midnight I was standing at the bow watching our massive loose linkage shudder as each wave came in when the messenger on watch brought a message that a cold front with high winds was expected at 0400. we stood there chewing over that item and in about 10 minutes the conn called to say our heading was slowly diminishing. (They had orders to advise of any change of as much as 1 degree.) The boat was ordered to stop pushing and just then with a great whoop the cold front arrived. I had started up to the conn as soon as the reverse swing started, but the initial gust was so hard that by the time I got up there, and before the boat could check the swing, swing, we had snapped the ramp-to-pontoon chains, carried away the bitts on the second pontoon, and except for one or two sets of chains the outboard pontoon was free of the middle one. As a very heavy rain began we closed the bow, heaved in on the stern anchor, cast off from the pontoon, used the boat to hold our head up, and when clear dropped the bow anchor. We sat between the two anchors, with a good strain on each, until the good old Seabees had induced their errant pontoon to quiet down. The weather became calmer in about an hour and the Seabees were able to start lacing the pontoons together again. They were ready by dawn so we reestablished connection and proceeded with the war.

Unloading ammunition at Okinawa via
pontoon causeway. (Adams, 2002)

791 was ordered to move down the beaches almost to the extreme right flank and anchor off white beach on April 2. She anchored in 33 fathoms with 325 feet of stern anchor cable played out. Preparations for launching the LCT commenced. This maneuver is dangerous as they would literally let the ship roll to one side as the smaller vessel would slide off the deck to the water on the down side of the ship. The crew first greased the timbers under the LCT, removing the side rails, life rafts and deck guns from the starboard side. Collision fenders had to be dropped over the side and secured. Next, flooding the starboard side ballast tanks and blowing the port tanks had to be done to achieve a 27 degree list to starboard. Retaining lines then had to be released and the LCT slide down the main deck and off the side of the ship at 2033 hours after which she was moored alongside. The keel was evened at 2233 hours and they completed transferring 5000 gallons of fresh water at 2315 hours. Following the LCT 828 crew then boarded her and at 0015 hours they started fueling her, transferring 3450 gallons of fuel which

was completed at 0210 hours. LCT 828 then departed. Her job helping land supplies and ferrying troops continued throughout the campaign.

Tenth Army consumed vast amounts of supplies. Over 577,000 tons of supplies landed on the Hagushi beaches between April 1 and 16. A major problem occurred on April 6, two ammunition ships, the Hobbs Victory and the Logan Victory, became targets and destroyed by kamikazes, severely limiting artillery ammunition supplies. Due to this loss on the 13 of April, General Buckner became upset to learn that only 640 tons of artillery ammunition had been landed. That stockpile of shells was not nearly enough for such a large expenditure of shells of all types. General Buckner then gave priority to artillery shells and within several days 3,000 tons per day had been deposited ashore. Also, for the fleet the matter of supply became acute and solved by a new class of LST ammunition ships equipped with cranes. These ships would shuttle between the Marianas, Ulithi and the Keramas bringing ammunition to the fleet and directly depositing the cargo on the decks of the warships. The 791 would help in ferrying 1,183 tons to Okinawa from Guam. Okinawa was not only a battle between two armies and navies, but a battle of supply.

April 2, 3, 4 they heard small arms fire, but did not see much enemy activity. The skipper, Lt. Duncan noted episodes that occurred during those days in the lull of the battle after securing the airfields. "On D plus 1 or D plus 2 the Japanese knew we had their airfields, but all the same a plane deliberately come into one. It was a single engine fighter plane with plenty of gas and ammunition. He strafed an LVT, setting it on fire, circled the field, and calmly landed. Our people stopped firing and covered him. The pilot got out, put his head down, and started running toward nowhere in particular. He was shot. The next day a fighter plane came in, strafed a pillbox, and landed. The pilot ran and was shot. Nobody here seems able to figure that out. Were the pilots saki'd up? Were they indulging in the Japanese gesture of contempt accomplished by committing hare kari on an enemy's doorstep? You guess; I just work here." (Adams, 2002) Indeed, another report from Yontan Airfield described a similar or the same event: as the American bulldozers busy clearing away wrecked enemy planes and dummy planes from the runway a plane with Japanese markings began approaching the field. Bulldozers fell silent and the Marines jumped to the ground clutching their weapons. Others occupied with preparing meals, stopped and made their way to the field weapons in hand. The zero swung out seaward in the landing pattern and got onto final and made a smooth landing. As the pilot pulled off his parachute pack and climbed down to the tarmac he sighted some soldiers at the edge of the field. He froze and then realized his predicament and grasped for his pistol. With what can only be described as horror realizing too late what he had done, he was simultaneously riddled with fusillade of Marine bullets. (Leckie, 1995)

Okinawa Invasion Beach from Inland (Naval History &Heritage Command)

LSTs would wait at anchor for a slot to unload during those crucial days. The ship with what had been considered "hot cargo" or supplies like ammunition had priority in unloading. The crew stood their watches and there even had been an attempt on the 4th to show a movie. However, the bulb went out on the projector which meant no movies at all until it was fixed and that time wasn't known. Skipper would remember on those quiet days, lone Jap planes had kept popping in and out of cloud cover over the beach, maybe sending a story home about the invasion. And sometimes they would be shot down. 791 was anchored in a new position [Uncle] and LCI 755 came alongside to starboard at 1642 hours to load 506 rounds of 4.2 H.E. mortar shells and then she departed.

This aerial view of the beachhead on L+4 (April 4) illustrates the logistical effort to maintain an invasion. Six LSTs are offloading at the center right of the photo. The reef prevents grounding to get closer to shore. The small bay above left of the LSTs is the mouth of the Bishi Gawa river. One of these LSTs maybe is the 791. (USMC National Archive)

On the 5 at 1235 hours an enemy midget submarine reported being sighted 2 miles off Point Bolo [Zampa Cape, the far western end of the invasion beaches]. The 791 was anchored at Green Beach #2 and

Point Bolo was on a bearing of 189 degrees and 5800 yards distant. A periscope also reported sighted 300 yards astern of the attack transport APA 71, USS Catron. Torpedoes had been reported to be in the water, but no hits recorded. Whether these reports described an actual event or report of some scared young American sailors' imagination conjuring up something that wasn't there doesn't mean that the danger of Japanese submarines didn't exist. Indeed, Japanese submarines formed to attack American shipping anchored at Okinawa. Four submarines the I-58, I-44, I- 47 and I-56 formed the "Tatara group" in the later part March of 1945. Some of them carried Kaitens, or suicide manned torpedoes. Due to intense anti-submarine defenses they largely failed to accomplish their mission. I-47 and the I-36 formed the "Tembu"[Heavenly Warriors] group on 20 April armed with six kaitens apiece. They had been ordered to attack American supply ships between Ulithi and Okinawa. Usually they reported back to Japan great successes, when in reality they had minimal to no success, or did they have any influence on the battle. But they indeed posed a threat, as the destruction of fleet oiler AO 59 Mississinewa by a Kaiten on 20 November 1944 in the anchorage at Ulithi made the U.S. command well aware of. I-58 went on to sink the cruiser USS Indianapolis after she delivered the atomic bomb to Saipan on July 30, 1945.

They hadn't seen any enemy planes for those couple days, but that changed. Kamikaze or the Special Attack concept of suicide attacks originated in the Philippines and Saipan. Early attacks in the war operated sporadically and ill organized at best. It wasn't until Okinawa that a well organized planned attack had been mounted; called Ten-Go Operation [or Heavenly Operation]. Admiral Soemu Toyoda commanded the 1st Special Attack Force of over 2,944 aircraft of the combined 5th Air Fleet and 6th Air Army based at Kyushu and Formosa. Planes of all types used, including the famous zero fighter or Zeke. The pilots of kamikazes received only very rudimentary training, just enough to take off, fly and die. Sometimes, the cockpits had been sealed after the pilot got seated. Bodies of kamikaze pilots would also be found in wreckage with parachute harnesses and flame retardant suits on. Limited attacks had been made during the initial landings, but the full force of this unit was not felt until a massive 355 plane raid on April 6 through 7. In 19 hours during those two days six ships were sunk, 21 damaged with over 500 casualties.

Weaver had the watch until midnight of the 5th. They had been anchored off Green Beach #2 in 22 fathoms of water with 110 fathoms of chain to the bow anchor. General Quarter's alarms sounded at 0330 hours on the 6th from a reported mass air raid and sea attack forming. Morning of the 6th dawned overcast with northeast winds moving layers of clouds along at three thousand to seven thousand foot altitudes. This provided good cover and therefore good suicide weather. The sea attack became the desperate sortie by the battleship Yamato on April 6th. She displaced over 71,600 tons and could attain the speed of 27 knots. More than 150 guns had been mounted on her with nine 18.1 inch naval rifles that could shoot a 3,200 lbs. shell over 22 miles. She was 863 feet long, with her bridge towering 80 feet above the deck and had the heaviest armor ever installed on a battleship making her all, but impregnable. This super battleship's mission to beach herself on Okinawa to the south of the landing beaches and turn her 18 inch guns loose on American forces ashore and the transports in the anchorage. She had only enough fuel for a one way trip. This had been Operation Ten-Ichi or Heaven Number One. Yamato had one light cruiser the Yahagi and eight destroyers as escorts. They sailed from Tokuyama Naval Base on southwest of Honshu. Overall command of this surface special attack force was under Vice-Admiral Seiichi Ito. One destroyer turned back with engine trouble, but later followed the task force. U.S. submarines SS-295 Hackleback and SS-410 Threadfin detected the Japanese force soon after it entered the open sea in the Bungo Strait area. They tried to get within torpedo range but thwarted by the escort. However they did give a series of contact reports to Pearl before being forced aside. This enabled the U. S. fleet to track her. Contact being lost during the night as the force turned west. Reconnaissance aircraft ducking in and out of clouds sighted her task group on April 7 after the Japanese task force turned southwest toward Okinawa. Then the aircraft of Task Force 58 found them striking at noon. Yamato sank after taking 10 torpedo and 5 bomb hits. Yahagi sank after 7 torpedoes and 12 bomb hits, along with four destroyers. This attack took 2 hours and cost ten U.S. aircraft. Four damaged escort destroyers escaped back to Japan. The last major naval effort by Japan had thus ended.

Yamato under attack by U.S. Navy Planes,
April 7, 1945 (National Archives)

The commander of the kamikaze air attacks waited until around noon on the 6th to launch. He hoped to catch the patrolling American fighters at their most vulnerable, refueling on carrier decks or on the aprons of the Yontan and Kadena airfields. A ruse of dropping window or chaff [strips of aluminum foil] to create false blips on radar screens to lure the defensive fighters away from the target had also been done. The Americans had deployed a wide circle of sixteen radar picket destroyers around the central hub of Point Bolo. Later in the day Japanese fighters arrived off Okinawa's airfields and had been intercepted by American fighters on patrol. At three o'clock the kamikazes struck. They dove on the radar pickets and concentrated on ships in the Hagushi anchorage. Over two hundred suicide planes came steadily for about five hours until darkness veiled the ships.

Beginning around 1615 hours, Weaver again had been in the LCVP when the enemy began to attack the harbor. As had been standard operating procedure smoke generators on almost all the ships in the anchorage started making smoke to screen themselves. He saw 10 enemy aircraft shot down during that attack with one being singled out by the 791. Stripe and Thornhill at their battle stations on the bow twin 40 along with almost every other crewman on the 791 could see squinting through the smoke a lone kamikaze among the gaggle of others in the air among flack bursts. It appeared to be singling out their ship or the nearby hospital ship as it began its death dive. They would concentrate on that menacing plane. The gun directors pointed at the target and the gun captains told their men to hold their fire until it got within range. They could see the big blood red balls on the light grey wings and fuselage. Then the order to fire was given! As the kamikaze continued in his death dive the crew realized that it had been the nearby hospital ship that had been picked as the target. The men manning the guns on the 791 realized they had to stop it before it reached that ship! Riley described that attack as: "the Jap came in from over the island and started down in a suicide dive on a hospital ship. The plane started to waffle and he put one wing down and crashed close to the [hospital] ship." (Riley, 1943-1945) The 791 had been the closest vessel to the hospital ship.

Robert Sherrod a TIME Correspondent had been observing the action from a landing boat. He watched and what he described as a twin engine Jap bomber sneak over a hillside and head into the fleet. He thought the kamikaze picked out a transport near his craft. He radioed; "The antiaircraft fire, 20 and 40 mm, seemed a solid flame of tracer shells, converging on him from a cone formed by a hundred ships. When he was about half a mile away he caught fire, started to roll over. What looked like an engine or a large piece of engine flew out and ricocheted along the water. The plane hit the water. Chunks of plane sailed past our boat. A stream of flame shot past a hospital ship nearby. Then the peril set in. Our own antiaircraft fragments started splashing around. I wished fervently that I had worn my helmet." (Sherrod, Robert, 1945)

The Reporters   May 8 1945

The attached clipping provoked many guffaws when the April 16 TIME turned up. The fellow who wrote this must have been hiding in the bilges of the landing boat, not looking out of it.

We were close enough to this incident to contribute some antiaircraft fire, and consequently feel some confidence in our observations. It wasn't a twin bomber. He didn't pick out a transport; he tried to crash-dive a hospital ship. (He just missed, too.) He didn't really throw one of his engines at the reporter, either. He didn't catch fire and start to roll over. He just put one wing down to adjust his course a little. You have to do that when you turn.

What got all of us was that the incident was dramatic enough in the most factual telling. Why these characters overlay their accounts with a lot of fantasy is beyond me. If he had sent home a factual narrative of what actually happened he would have had a good story.

One of the little fantasies we indulge in from time to time is the idea of an invasion the first wave of which would consist entirely of reporters and cameramen. As you can imagine, we embroider and embellish this concept with great pleasure.

We felt ever so badly about Ernie Pyle. H e is the one reporter who we felt was one of us.

It made me feel sort of good to know he was going to be at Okinawa. We found it out at Ulithi; he was there too. Most of us took a very personal interest in him, and considered him a semi-acquaintance. I suppose that is particularly true of those who had been in an operation with him. I think his stature will increase rather than diminish. Certainly he will be remembered with great affection by a lot of fighting men.

Action report for that day stated that the 791 lay at anchor in the mid northwestern part of the anchorage [Green Beach #2 area]. The kamikaze had been a Val first picked up by sight at less than 5 miles. Japanese Navy's main and last fixed gear dive bomber used early in the war had been the Aichi D3A Val. D3A2's had been utilized extensively during the last year of the war in kamikaze operations as they could be stabilized in their death dives by the bomber's dive brakes. It had a range of around 900 miles and maximum speed of 266 mph at 20,000 feet altitude. The bomber could carry approximately 700 lbs of bombs.

The Val approached at an altitude of 1000 feet and its speed estimated to be 100 knots. It had been tracked for 7 seconds before being fired on by six of the ship's 40 mm and two of the 20 mms. Hits started being recorded at 1830:41 hours at a range of 2000 yards and a bearing of 45 degrees. Last shot, 25 seconds later, hit the plane at 1500 yards at a bearing of 175 degrees from the 791 and the Val was 300 feet above the water. Effectiveness of the gunnery s reported as "fairly good" with hits being observed. The sun was to port (left) with the 791 bow angled toward the north and the beaches. Which meant the kamikaze was flying into the sun and could be seen clearly by crew of 791. During this one plane's attack 226 rounds of 40 mm ammunition and 150 rounds of 20 mm ammunition or just 4% of the ships total ammunition reserve was expended. The crew of the 791 has always believed they had been the ones that shot that kamikaze down and saved the hospital ship.

Japanese Aichi D3A Val Dive Bomber (Scott Nelson 2011)

April 6, 1945, LST 791 anchored in front of the USS Comfort just off Green Beach 2 (Scott Nelson, 2011)

Two hospital ships had been among the fleet on April 2 through the 9, USS Comfort [AH-6] and USS Relief [AH-1]. Comfort was the target of that kamikaze and she was anchored behind the 791. A report from the USS Comfort says the plane appeared to be headed for the hospital ship. The intense fire from the nearby ships sheared off a wing and the plane went out of control landing in the water yards from the bow of the Comfort. (Harper, 2001) On April 9 at 0445 and 0452 hours an enemy plane attempted to bomb the Comfort with two bombs, both missing by only 50 yards. There had been also eight LST[H]s lying at anchor or beached at the Hagushi invasion beeches that day.

BHAlmy Charles Finger, Gene Joyce, SC Walters, RR Meshuret RJ Crane, J Donnelly, HA Dulumba

Aft(stern) 40mm gun crew. (Morley, 2003–2005)

Max Stripe (left) and Billy Thornhill (right) at their twin 40mm mount after the 791 shot down a kamikaze at Okinawa. (Stripe-Bruhn, 2003-2010)

Bow Twin 40 mm mount at standby battle stations. (Morley, 2003-2005)

Hospital ships did become prime targets of kamikazes, the big Red Cross's making a beautiful aiming point for enemy pilots. Indeed, during the battle on April 27, at 10:41 pm the Hospital ship U.S.S. Comfort had been deliberately attacked again. Comfort had been sailing fifty miles southwest of Okinawa with a full load of casualties [#700] on a clear night in the presence of a full moon. According to Geneva Convention protocol she had been lighted and off limits to attack. The kamikaze hit the ship and crashed through three superstructure decks prior to exploding in surgery. Twenty nine had been killed, including 6 surgeons and 6 nurses operating at the time with other operating room personnel. Forty nine others had sustained wounds. The skipper; Commander Adin Tooker took precautions while the fires and flooding had been dealt with. He swung out undamaged lifeboats and darkened the ship. He also asked the commander of Task Force at Okinawa to provide ships for anti-aircraft screen in case the enemy wanted to finish the job. At the Okinawa anchorage ships, especially LSTs, due to their large capacity tank decks, had been ordered to stand by in case they became needed for a rescue mission to the Comfort. Tooker's crew was able to make repairs to get underway to Guam and arrived safely five days later.

Part of the kamikaze attack plan included suicide speed boats. Saipan is where improvised suicide boats using landing barges and captured allied boats began and had some successes. The result was the purpose built suicide boats used at Okinawa. Navy boats known as Shinyo [Ocean Shaker] had 595 lbs explosive in the bow and designed to ram enemy vessels. Army boats, known as Maru-re [Liaison Boat], armed with two 264 lbs depth charges and designed to get in close and drop the charges near their targets. Altogether they became known as Q-boats to American forces and referred to at Imperial Headquarters as Renraku-tai [Liaison Unit]. These little craft represented real threats. The suicide boats had been organized into boat battalions of about seventy five to one hundred boats with one hundred to one hundred and fifty men per battalion. These boats measured 16 ft. long by 5 ft. wide to 21 ft. long by 6 ft wide and made of plywood. Q-boats powered by various motors and could reach 20 to 25 knots for a range of 3 and ½ hours. Manned by 15 to 17 year old 2nd and 3rd year officer cadets of the officer academies and if they failed to return after a mission they then got promoted posthumously to lieutenant. They meant to sever the American supply lines by ramming into supply convoy ships and blowing up.

A Shinyo found on Aka Jima, Kerama Retto. A marine stands guard near where they were found hidden in caves and transported to the water on trailers. (USMC)

Three of these Q-boat battalions of Army Maru-re had been based in the Kerama Retto islands, a cluster of nine islands 15 miles southeast of the main island of Okinawa. Lt. Duncan remarked that "the islands appear to be a group of sunken mountains, with their tops sticking out of the water. They are wooded and, as intelligence report would say, afford excellent concealment for a defending force." (Adams, 2002) On March 26-27 an invasion by the Army 77th Infantry Division, effectively neutralizing the suicide boats and secured the supply lines. About 250 of these one man boats had been found in well camouflaged inlets. Personnel of the Maru-re battalions retreated to the hills and conducted harassment operations until the end of hostilities.

Naval personnel inspecting a Maru-re type 5 at Kerama Retto on April 10. The racks just behind the pilot held two depth charges. In attacking a target the pilot would swerve next to the ship and drop the charges that would be set to explode at shallow depth and blow a hole in the hull of the ship. (U.S. Navy)

Lt. Duncan described what happened on the largest of the Kerama Retto islands: "On the largest island are between 600 and 800 well organized Japanese. Two captured Japanese volunteered to go in and talk to them about surrender. They stopped at a native village at one end of the island and got a couple ladies to accompany them. Upon arriving at Japanese HQ, the heads of all four were carefully detached and returned to the native village. So the word has been passed, as we say, that the garrison means to fight. We have since learned that they expect to be able to hold on until Nippon wins the war and comes back to relieve them. They think it is just a question of time. Some of the islands we hold have snipers. Those who go far from the beach alone have a good chance of not returning." (Adams, 2002)

Four other Maru-re suicide boat battalions operated, mainly at night, from southern Okinawa itself and had limited, if any success. Usually intercepted by PT boats and by alert shipboard guards they prevented any significant damage to the fleet. The only damage done by them during the battle was sinking a LCI, damaging two destroyers and damaging a LCS[L]. During the battle the Kerama Retto islands became the fleet's refueling, rearming and repair base.

The Landing Craft Support [LCS(L)] was used primarily for close support before landing on the beaches. These highly armed 158 foot long vessels earned the nickname "mighty midgets" for their array of weapons; a single 3 inch gun, two or three twin 40 mms, four 20 mms, four .50 cal machine guns and ten MK 7 rocket launchers. They had been manned by 3-6 officers and around 60 enlisted men. They also performed as antiaircraft escorts for radar picket destroyers, created smoke to hide the fleet at anchor and perform patrol duties screening for suicide boats.

Ships at anchor also had to post guards, armed with rifles and pistols to guard against Japanese suicide swimmers. It was said among U.S. crews that sometimes someone would come across small patrol boats with dead crews who had their throats slashed. They also carried explosives and would attack full size ships. An example is the attack of the LCI 404 patrolling in the Palau islands. The suicide swimmers approached the ship's bow and stern with charges. All hands including the skipper became involved in shooting the attackers. All had been killed except for one seen to dive beneath the stern. An explosion rocked the steering engine room. Damage control kept the ship afloat. Soon afterwards the crewmen of the LCI sighted and destroyed an enemy raft two hundred feet astern. This desperate strategy was also used in the Philippines among other islands.

Attacks continued unabated with a total of 14 allied ships sunk and 90 damaged through April by kamikazes. Conventional attacks also occurred with one ship sunk and 47 damaged. May saw more attacks concentrating on picket ships, transports, carriers and allied airfields. The attacks continued to the end of the Okinawa campaign with the last on 21-22 of June. There had been 10 main attacks in total, interspersed with smaller ones involving around 2,500 kamikaze aircraft and five times that number in conventional aircraft attacks. Each main attack became known as Kikusui [floating chrysanthemum] #1 through Kikusui #10. Kikusui #1 was the largest with 230 kamikazes from the Navy, 125 kamikazes from the Army and supported by 344 conventional aircraft. Twenty six U.S. ships total had been sunk and 225 damaged by kamikazes during the battle of Okinawa. Two ships had been sunk and 61 others damaged by conventional attack. These attacks produced the highest U.S. Navy casualty rate of the war, 4,907 killed and 4,824 wounded. 763 U.S. aircraft had been lost during the campaign. The invasion of Okinawa is the costliest battle in naval history. Suicide attacks are a desperation tactic. Their effectiveness on U.S. forces has been and will be debated. What will not be debated is the psychological effect on the servicemen at the front and on the families at the home front.

The Special Attack Corps

You have probably read in magazines about the Kamikaze, or Special Attack Corps. This is a group of earnest young Nipponese who have as their primary ambition diving their planes into American ships. It seems quite a cold-blooded pursuit at first blush, and of course when you see these gentlemen in action the lethal nature of their intentions is graphically impressed upon one.

Well, you know a lot of gossip goes around during a war even as during peace. One of the items is that a plane tried to crash one of our battleships and missed, crashing in the water close aboard. Surprising enough, the pilot lived a little while. He turned out to be fifteen years old. He had 60 hours of flying time. He had a flame-resistant suit so if his plane caught fire he could pilot it to its objective anyway. Now when I see one of these misguided citizens I do not have an uncontrollable impulse to order the guns to hold their fire. Do not get the wrong idea. Nevertheless I have never cheered when an enemy plane fell, and now when one of those chaps goes down I can't help thinking of some of the.15-year old boys I know. A plane itself, like a ship, seems pretty impersonal, but there may be in that Jap plane a scared little undernourished 15- year old boy. He's all hopped up with a lot of stuff about the divinity of the Emperor, and of course he has had a snappy funeral and send-off, but I have an idea that when the tracers start reaching up toward him he's just a scared kid. Once I saw one--in the April 6th attack on the invasion forces at Okinawa--make a bee-line for a hospital ship. He took plenty of punishment going in, but they just knocked him down a hundred or so yards short of the ship. Of course that doesn't stimulate any springs of compassion for the pilot. Surely though if we could arrange to bring that lad up right he would be of some use to the world. He might not exactly be a second Pasteur or Lister, but at least he probably wouldn't be going around in an airplane trying to knock off a lot of guys who are already wounded and can't take very good care of themselves anyway. From the little I have seen of the suicide planes, which is not enough to qualify me as an authority, I would say they are overrated as a menace. Of course a certain number of them may get through to hit an objective, like bombs do, but their average doesn't seem very high. A modern ship can throw up an awful lot of lead.

April 7th found the 791 beached on the edge of a reef at Red Beach Three and commenced unloading operations, including disembarking eleven men. April 8th nothing unusual happened, though they did have general quarters at 0400 hours, no planes appeared however. They completed unloading operations early on the 8th. They then moved to within 7500 yards of Point Bolo and LST 947 moored alongside to starboard to unload 1500 rounds of mortar shells onto the 791. On the 9th they had been moored alongside to LST 926 and received 150 rounds of 4.2 mortar shells, 300 fuses and 208 5 inch shells. LCT-1050 moored alongside after LST 926 left and they fueled her. They then shifted anchorage and went to G.Q. On the 10th G.Q. was sounded at 0526 hours and afterwards they made preparations for getting underway and moored alongside LST 622 in berth 119 and unloaded 2700 rounds of H.E. mortar shells and 600 rounds of white phosphorus mortar shells onto the moored LST. They also unloaded smoke materials, 15 drums of fog oil and 20 floating smoke pots and then made preparations to get underway. On the 11th they had left Okinawa and Weaver said he was happy because he could get some sleep. Their destination was Saipan. April 13th Lt. Adams was Officer of the Deck on the bridge when he heard the convoy commander send a message: "Bogey bearing 090, 1000 yards." (Adams, 2002) The next message after asking for the first to be repeated by Lt. Adams was; "Bogey bearing 270, 1000 yards." (Adams, 2002) The kamikaze passed right over the convoy, but could not see the ships due to cloud cover. With the decks clear and the convoy at sea, another large raid occurred at Okinawa on the 11th. During that raid 118 Jap planes were shot down and the allies lost 15 ships. The skipper held Captains Mass on the 15th after hearing news about the death of President Roosevelt on April 12. Most of the crew expressed sorrow as they grew up knowing no other president.

Arriving at Saipan on the 17th, Weaver got small boat duty again and had it almost every day while there. Assistant surgeon John Pritchett USPHS Reserve reported aboard for duty. On the 18th moored alongside LST 790 they took on 40,000 gallons of fuel and 17,400 gallons of water. After which they moved to a different berth. A storm warning had been issued on the 22nd. Maintenance was done on the 24th scrapping the deck. Pay was distributed to the crew, coming to around $85/seaman. The fresh water evaporator broke down. It became the black gangs' responsibility to install a spare. This job fell to Charles Berlau, James Hill and Charlie Haight and they worked feverishly to get this important piece of equipment operational again. Until completed they had to have all of their fresh water stores replenished from AO-61, USS Severn [fleet oiler] and received 61,276 gallons. 25th of April machinist C. H. Higgins Jr. was transferred ashore for transport to the states. Liberty had been granted to Weavers section on the 27th, but he couldn't go because he still had small boat duty. C. W. Keck MoMM1c was transferred to the Naval Hospital on Saipan per verbal orders of the skipper. Then an inspection of the men and ship was held on the 28th. Finally on the 29th Weaver got out of small boat duty. May 1st they painted the main deck forward and Weaver got assigned to the mess for the next month. May 3rd they left for Guam arriving there at Apra Harbor Guam on the 4th at 1655 hours and moored starboard side to LST 866 in berth 13. Then got underway for LST North Landing Apra Harbor and beached and commenced loading "1183 tons of plain and fancy explosives". (Adams, 2002) The 791 attempted to retract on the 7th. R. Farrow S2c was transferred to the U. S. Naval Base Hospital for treatment. PhoM3c J. W. Papsun reported aboard.

The Marianas are made up of 15 islands and only three had been invaded and occupied by the United States; Saipan, Tinian and Guam.

All three had seen brutal combat in their taking by force, but during the visit of the 791 they had become major bases. As bases they had been built up with acres of new warehouses, administration buildings, airfields, harbors, training facilities, roadways, hospitals and barracks to house thousands of servicemen. They also became recreational paradises with outdoor movie theaters, softball diamonds, basketball courts, boxing rings in arenas and radio stations to provide music, news and other shows. Guam became the headquarters of U. S. Fleet in the central Pacific.

Lt. Duncan remembered Saipan and Guam: "Saipan is not an atoll, but a real island. There are coral reefs around it but it sticks right up above the water and bears trees which are not palm trees and in general looks like a self-respecting piece of land. There is no more sand than you find on any beach. After seeing many atolls in the course of some months it is significant to report that you can't look right across Saipan to the sea on the other side. There are still some Japanese wandering about the island and they sometimes take a potshot at anyone foolish enough to go up into the hills. But the last time I heard a rumor concerning the subject it seemed that there was a big roundup on and there was considerable whacking of shrubbery to get the Nips out of their cover. We were at Saipan about two weeks, and then moved down to Guam for a few days." (Adams, 2002)

He went on about Guam: "Little Pearl, as the more erudite call it, has asphalt roads with signs such as "GUAM", like in the States. A cultural note indicating the degree to which civilization has pushed back the jungle is the fact that one of Guam's hills is called Flush-toilet Hill, this area having the only flush toilets west of Pearl. Guam is a scene of much activity. There is sufficient rank around so that there are many regulations. The result is that Saipan is much preferred. But both places are pretty quiet and good for seeing a lot of your friends." (Adams, 2002) Japanese had been prodded out of areas of Guam form time to time and it was said that within two hours of a ship getting to Guam, Tokyo Rose would broadcast it was there and promised to bomb it. Rota an island between Guam and Saipan was still held by the Japanese and allied bombers would use it for target practice from time to time.

One of the coxswains was sentenced to the brig for 3 days for some infraction on the 7th. Discipline was a task that was a continuous process on the ship. All the crew had been either in their late teens or early twenties, with the officers not much older, and they still had that adolescent indiscipline streak in them. Usual trail of events was being put on report for some breach of duty or infraction of the rules. The range of ill deeds could range from being late back from liberty [AOL or AWOL, Absent With Out Leave], not reporting or being late for watch or drill, excessive use of water for showers, not reporting an incident like a malfunction in the ships communications equipment promptly, disobeying an officer or petty officer, disobeying a SP, having someone else's possessions, insubordination, being asleep on watch, inattention at duty, leaving post without permission, and scandalous conduct tending to destruction of good morals. A Captain's mast [the Captain hears the case and decides the punishment] was then usually held or in the extreme a deck trial or summary court marshal was held rarely. Most punishments consisted of reprimands. But, it could also include extra duty in hours or days, loss of future liberties, probation and being put in the brig or in solitary confinement for a period of time, with or without bread and water as the only food and drink. In extreme cases and very rare indeed a crewman could be transferred off the ship. But by far the majority of the crew did their duty promptly and earnestly.

Most of the crew passed the time off duty by reading and playing games. Alcohol, primarily beer could generally be obtained on liberty or at points of R and R [Relaxation and Recreation]. General order 99 of 1914 strictly prohibited "the use or introduction for drinking purposes of alcoholic liquors on board any naval vessel, or within any navy yard or station, is strictly prohibited, and commanding officers will be held directly responsible for the enforcement of this order." At times beer and other spirits had been smuggled on board by enlisted men as well as officers for celebrations and toasts to the fallen. Very few commanding officers made it an issue. But it was a directive that begged to be broken. Gambling always had been a pastime. The officers generally ignored most of these, if they knew about them, as long as the activities did not interfere with the operations of the ship or its safety. They assumed that it was good for morale.

Guam

Little Pearl, as the more erudite call it, has asphalt roads with signs such as GUAM like in the States. A cultural note indicating the degree to which civilization has pushed back the jungle is the fact that one of Guam's hills is called Flush-toilet Hill, this area housing the only flush toilets west of Pearl.

Guam is the scene of much activity. There is sufficient amount of rank around so that there are many regulations. The result is that Saipan is much preferred. But both places are pretty quiet and good for seeing a lot of your friends. Phil Peltz, Jimmy Mulligan, and Bill Cain were at Saipan. Don Taylor, Frank Canker, and Al Brodkin were at Guam. Barry Bingham was at Ulithi when we were in Guam (20 June). Dave McCandless apparently left Saipan just before I got a chance to see him.

There are some Chamarro's on Guam and Saipan. There is a story that the ladies of this breed have what are sometimes termed loose ways. Personally I see no reason for criticizing friendship in an area where there hasn't been much of it lately.

However, even a young and ignorant Marine would have to be out here quite a long time before he would be attracted by a Chamarro charmer. Or so I would think. Japs are still prodded out of the Guamanian hinterland from time to there. They apparently have pretty good intelligence It is said that within two hours after a certain ship got to Guam Tokyo Rose said it was there and charitably promised to bomb it. I was in Guam when that happened; it seems to be accepted as true. But they didn't bomb it.

Rota, between Guam and Saipan, is still held by the Japs. Our bombers use it for practice work. What a job - being a practice target. "Hold still, please."

Tokyo Rose

Tokyo Rose is a stupid dolly with an unattractive voice and an unimaginative script writer. Whereas Midge, who used to broadcast from Radio Berlin, had a very nice voice, an excellent delivery, and a cleverly insinuating script that kept you guessing about just how much the Jerries knew about what you were doing. Of course I have nothing against this female and am sure she is doing her best. Maybe it is her sponsor's fault. But when General Patton gets to Berlin I think it would be nice if he would send Midge (sometimes called Mazie) to Tokyo to be a guest star on Rose's program. It would not affect the Emperor's war potential very much and when you get so close to Japan that their stations come in better than your own it is only fair that we should improve the quality of their offerings.

The Nip intelligence is pretty good, but they present their scoops in such a dull way as to give you the minimum amount of creeps. For instance, Rosie sounded off well back in March about our plans to go to Okinawa. But whereas the Fuhrer's sound effects staff would have given us a good case of goose-pimples and had us looking over our shoulders for a couple of days, Rosie was much less effective. She just blurted out that so many of Admiral Mitscher's ships had been sunk off the Japanese coast the Okinawa operation would have to be delayed. You can tease people by radio, and you can arouse their curiosity and apprehension, but you can't club them to death.

Furthermore, Radio Tokyo's music is very corny. It is semi- classical, apparently played by some broken-down refugees from Jimmy Petrillo.

I am not exactly beefing, you understand. The Rome station was no great shakes and sometimes I think WFIW and WHAS leave something to be desired. But when the recreational facilities are as limited as they are out here, it does seem to me that the, people in charge ought to try a little harder.

They left for Saipan on the 9th at 1800 hours after navy personnel reported aboard for transportation. The 791 took up one of the positions in a small convoy of two other LST's and few escorts with the tug YTL-426 in tow. Arriving at 0832 hours and linked up with APA-206, USS Sibley [attack transport] and commenced taking on 31,915 gallons of fresh water. They received word of the German surrender on May 8th with little celebration; most had been concerned with their own war in the pacific. Some thought at least it might free up more men to help end the war against Japan. Riley noted in his diary: "Now that the war is over in Europe and we can concentrate entirely on Japan, it shouldn't take quite so long to finish them off. Maybe not this year, but by sometime next year we may all be home again." (Riley, 1943-1945) Several G.Q. had been called during the voyage with an escort dropped depth charges on a sub following the convoy on the 17th. They stood general quarters most of the day and night as they drew closer to Okinawa. On the 19th they arrived back at Okinawa and at 0920 lost electrical power due to the governor on the auxiliary engine failing. It had to be repaired promptly. The tug tow lines had been cast off and the navy personnel were disembarked. On the 20th they moored to Causeway "A" at Purple Beach 2 and commenced unloading operations. Mail was also hauled and that was dispatched to the Fleet Post Office. At 1838 hours the alarm for G.Q. was sounded and they commenced making smoke. At 2020 they secured from G.Q. The 21st was Weaver's birthday and he noted: "just look where I am and still on Okinawa." (Weaver, 1943-1945) Mail call was the following day. The 21st saw them move to Causeway Able Purple Beach 2 and continue to unload ammunition. At 2200 hours on the 24th an air raid occurred, Jap planes flew over and dropped bombs ¼ mile from them. 791 guns couldn't reach them and the rest of May they had daily G. Q. sounded. They completed unloading on the 24th. Commissary stores had been received on the 31st. On the 31st orders had been received to make for Ie Shima and report to Island Government Command.

Saipan

Saipan is not an atoll but is a real island. There are coral reefs around it but it sticks right up above the water and bears trees which are not palm trees and in general looks like a self-respecting piece of land. There is no more sand than you would find on any beach. After seeing many atolls in the course of some months it is significant to report that you can't looks right across Saipan to the sea on the other side. We have moved in and enlarged the air fields greatly, as well as constructing roads and improving the harbor facilities. It still isn't what a civilized sailor would call a harbor, but at least it is a place where you can lie in the lee of the land if the wind blows from the right direction. If it blows from the wrong direction you get the hook up to prevent being set on shore.

There are still some Japanese wandering about the island and they sometimes take a potshot at any one foolish enough to go up into the hills. But the last time I heard a rumor concerning the subject it seemed that there was a big roundup on and there was considerable whacking of shrubbery to get the Nips out of their cover. We were at Saipan about two weeks, then moved down to Guam for a few days.

BEACHED WITHIN SIGHT OF WHERE ERNIE PYLE DIED

June 1st they left Okinawa for Ie Shima and arrived on the same day. 791 spent ten days at various anchor points around the island making smoke to screen other ships and acting as an antiaircraft battery. The triangle of ocean bounded by Ie Shima, Kerama Retto and the shore of Okinawa became known as "Kamikaze Gulch" (Gandt, 2010). The smoke machine would constantly catch on fire; necessitating a nozzle to be rigged above it to spray water onto the device. Crew was constantly at general quarters and frequently firing at kamikazes through smoke finding it nerve wracking and fatiguing. The skipper made some observations of Japanese planes: "Several times I have watched Japanese planes in the rays of search lights. The first time, the character up in the sky just cruised along looking around. A twin engine bomber, he went right over the transport area with all the large caliber guns in the place blazing away at him. He was quite high, but within range. He took no evasive action at all. The shooting was pretty bad; he went home. As far as we know he never drop any bombs. What impressed us was the way he just streamed along in a straight line. Another Jap tried the same thing sometime later and took a slug. He put the nose right down so as to get where he was going in a hurry. About half way down there was an explosion and he shed a few pieces. The plane fell harmlessly into the water. If he had been aiming for someone, I guess the explosion threw him off the target. But the question is, why don't they take evasive action?" (Adams, 2002) June 5th LCI-1093 came alongside for fueling and an air raid occurred during operations. They had to stop and the two ships parted. After the raid was over and G.Q. was secured the LCI returned to finish fueling. An airfield was nearby and the crew would watch flights of P-38s from the 318th Fighter Group and P-47s from the 413th Fighter Group take off and land. Some of the planes returning from battle would roll once per victory as they flew over the field.

791 beached at one location that was within a hundred yards from where the famous Pulitzer Prize winning 45 year old war correspondent Ernie Pyle had been killed. He worked for the Scripps-Howard newspaper chain and had covered the war in Europe from North Africa to Sicily, Italy and France. The beaches at Normandy saw him in the midst of the carnage. His reports about the average GI Joe endeared him to not only servicemen everywhere, but also to the folks back home. In fact a movie, "The Story of GI Joe", was tangentially about him, starring Burgess Meredith as Ernie Pyle and Robert Mitchum as a lieutenant premiered two months to the day after he was killed. He was reluctant to go back into combat, but figured he owed it to the boys in the Pacific. He made his way to Guam and then to Saipan. There he spent some time with B-29 crews, but grew restless. Then he spent some time on the escort carrier USS Cabot, but he wanted to see action and be with the soldiers and marines. He wrangled his way into a LVT with the marines heading for a northern sector of the invasion beaches code named "Yellow One" on April 1. He stayed for a few days realizing with the others that the

invasion of the beaches was too easy. He returned to the command ship USS Panamint. He learned of FDRs death there on April 12 and penned a few words. The Panamint was the headquarters ship for the Army's 77th Division and its assignment was to take the air strip on the ten square mile island of Ie Shima set for April 16. Ernie heard about a new tank destroyer being used on the island and wanted to take a look. April 17th he went ashore and spent the night in a Japanese ammunition bunker. He was to hitch a ride with Colonel Joseph Coolidge, the commanding officer of the 305 regiment, as he was about to cross the island to find a new site for the regimental command post the next day. The fighting was inland and the road from the beach was said to be quiet.

On the 18th of April Lt. Col. Joseph B. Coolidge with Ernie and three other soldiers had set out in a jeep along a road that paralleled the beach in a convoy of three trucks and a MP [military police] vehicle. As the jeep reached a road junction in the vicinity of Ie town, a machine gun opened up from a coral ridge about 1/3 mile away ahead of them. The jeep came to a screeching halt in a ditch after being hit in the tires and radiator. The soldiers with Ernie dived into that ditch. Pyle was next to Coolidge and they raised their heads to look around for the others. When Ernie saw that the others were safe he smiled and asked Coolidge: "Are you alright?" At that moment the enemy machine gunner opened fire again and struck Ernie in the left temple. He died instantly. Ernie was buried with his helmet on in a long row of graves among the soldiers, an infantry private on one side and an engineer on the other. (Pyle, 2008; Miller, 1950)

Lt. Duncan recorded his thoughts about Ernie. "We felt ever so badly about Ernie Pyle. He is the one reporter who we felt was one of us. It made me feel sort of good to know he was going to be at Okinawa. We found it out at Ulithi; he was there, too. Most of us took a very personal interest in him, and considered him a semi acquaintance. I suppose that is particularly true of those who had been in an operation with him. I think his stature will increase rather than diminish. Certainly he will be remembered with great affection by a lot of fighting men." (Adams, 2002)

He later had to be reburied in an Army Cemetery on Okinawa and then moved to the National Memorial Cemetery of the Pacific in Hawaii. Ernie Pyle Memorial on Okinawa became one of three American memorials that had been allowed to remain after Okinawa returned to Japanese control in 1972. (Miller, 1950) (Pyle, 2008) The monument read: "On this spot, the 77th Infantry Division lost a buddy, Ernie Pyle, 18 April 1945."

The Suburbs of Okinawa

As you have undoubtedly gathered, there are a number of small islands near Okinawa, which seem characteristic of the Ryukyu chain. We have been lucky enough to see most of the ones we hold, in the course of doing a few odd jobs subsequent to the initial phase of the operation. Ones we have seen are Ie Shima, Kerama Retto, Iheya and Aguni.

Ie Shima lies off Motobu Peninsula, part of Okinawa. It is off the northwest coast. All of the above islands are in the East China Sea. It is best known for being the place where Ernie Pyle was killed. There were still a few snipers hanging around (none swiped at us). There's nothing distinctive about the place.

Iheya is next, geographically. It is really quite pretty. There are smaller islands around it. Of course you have seen newspaper charts of all of these. We took Iheya without opposition. There had been some Japs there, but they apparently considered defense impracticable and went to Okinawa in boats after the shooting began on Okinawa. Some of them probably got through.

There is much disease and malnutrition among the natives on Iheya. Aguni lies off to the west of the Hagushi area of Okinawa, where the original landings were made. It has a fairly nice cliff on one end, but is otherwise undistinguished. It has the customary reef around it.

Kerma Retto is south and west of Haguishi. It provides quite the most striking scenery we have seen in the Pacific to date. It seems to be a group of sunken mountains, with their tops sticking out of the water. They are wooded and, as an intelligence report would say, "afford excellent concealment for a defending force." Mist hangs around the tops of the hills and the general impression is reminiscent of the Trossachs. On the largest island are 6 or 800 well-organized Japs. Two captured Japs volunteered to go in and talk to them about surrender. They stopped at a native village at one end of the island and got a couple of ladies to accompany them. Upon arriving at Jap HQ the heads of all four were carefully detached and returned to the native village. So the word has been passed, as we say, that the garrison means to fight. We have since learned that they expect to be able to hold on until Nippon wins the war and comes back to relieve them. They think it's just a question of time. Some of the islands we hold have snipers. Those who go far from the beach alone have a good chance of not returning. But they are cleaned out. We saw a pretty little shrine on one island. It is mined; stay away.

The story about the children blowing themselves and a few of our people up on one of the islands of Kerama Retto seems to be true.

I thought it was very pitiful. The children on Okinawa were cute. However, I didn't try to take any back to the ship. There was a Jap poem in TIME about the children on Kerama Retto. I guess the guy who told them whatever you tell children to make them do such things is a Jap hero. What a bunch of bastards.

Andy:

I had the mail Censor look over your letter (note his stamp and initials). I t' s O.K. for mailing but cannot be published or broadcast, as a matter of fact it must have that fact indicated on the letter.

Suggest the letter you use the wording I had put a t the bottom of when are you going to pay us another visit?

(s) Erank Cankar
P.S. My new phone no. is (Atlanta 5112)

LST 808

◇◇◇◇◇◇

On Ie Shima the crew sent a salvage party over to the wrecked LST 808 to retrieve two .50 caliber machine guns. The crew boasted that with those machine guns that would make the 791 one of the most heavily armed LSTs in the Pacific. This had been a common practice in the pacific; crews would add guns or make modifications to their ships. Salvaged and scrounged weapons from wrecked ships would find their way aboard and installed. She eventually had 22 guns; eight 40 mm, twelve 20 mm along with the two .50s from the 808. Two extra 20 mm had been stowed away below decks ready to be installed.

LST 808 beached on the 18th of May. At 2206 hours a large twin engine Japanese plane passed over the stern just above the mast, thirty seconds later a torpedo slammed into the ship with a powerful explosion. It killed five men and wounded five others, but the fires had been quickly extinguished. Five other men from the boat pool died in the explosion and one wounded man died the next day. With her main and auxiliary engine rooms demolished and flooded she had to be towed to shallow water where she rested on a reef. The majority of the crew went ashore on the 19th at 0300 hours. On the 20th there only five men on board when a kamikaze struck. At the time she was supplying fresh water and fog oil to the picket ships. The damage report of the air raid states: "while the ship was resting on the reef at Ie Shima, a Japanese plane dove into the forward part of the superstructure at 1837 hours and penetrated through the boat deck, main deck, and into the wreckage of the tank deck."

The 808 and LST 447 had been the only LSTs lost during the Okinawa campaign due to kamikaze action. The 447 had landed her cargo at the Hagushi beachhead and heading to anchorage near Kerama Retto. A Zeke crashed into her on April 6 with its bomb exploding below decks. Her fires could not be controlled and she had to be ordered abandoned. She burned for one day and finally sank. She suffered 5 killed and 21 wounded. Three other LST's had been damaged by kamikazes at Okinawa, they had been the 884 on April 1 with 24 crewman killed and 21 wounded; the 599 on April 3, with 21 men wounded; and 534 on June 22nd with 3 killed and 35 wounded. LST 808 was at Iwo Jima from February 15 to March 16th before she participated in Operation Iceberg. She was taken off the Navy roster and destroyed on November 11, 1945. From 1942 to 1945 a total of 41 LSTs had been lost in all theaters of war due to all causes. Twenty seven had been lost directly due to enemy action. *Photo: Ie Shima and LST 808 grounded during salvage of .50 cal machine guns. (Morley, 2003-2005)*

Photo: Ie Shima and LST 808 grounded during salvage of .50 cal machine guns. (Morley, 2003-2005)

LST 808 on fire after being torpedoed off Ie Shima. (National Archives)

Grounded LST 808 as seen from 791 just before the crew
salvaged the .50 cal machine guns. (Morley, 2003-2005)

FINAL PHASE OF OKINAWA OPERATIONS

On the 8th of June they had another air raid and it was noted that 38 raids had occurred in 24 hours and they had 135 contacts. With the help of a tug they beached at Red Tare 4 on the 11th and commenced loading vehicles and personnel of the Army 44th AAA Group. They left Ie Shima for the Kerama Retto anchorage at 1122 hours arriving there at 1611hours at berth King during an air attack. They then moved to Aka Kaikyo, Kerema Retto. From there to a pontoon causeway off Shirono Saki, Zamami Shima, Kerama Retto and commenced disembarking troops and vehicles at 1055 hours. They then returned to Okinawa and anchored in berth How off the invasion beaches on the 12 of June. As they came into the harbor they found a Jap body floating on the surface. They hoisted the body aboard, put chains around him and then cut the rope to sink him. It became fairly common for allied ships to find floating Japanese airmen. Many came from kamikaze escort fighters or guide planes. They either bailed out or crashed landed in the water.

They left for Iheya Jima to pick up L.V.T.'s on the 13th. Iheya Jima and Aguni Shima are islands north west of Okinawa. At the time of the campaign those islands became occupied. On the 3rd of June the 2nd and 3rd Battalions of the 8nd Marine Regiment of the 2th Marine Division landed on those two islands. Lt. Duncan commented on the operation at Iheya and Aguni: "There's nothing distinctive about the place. Ihey is next, geographically. It is really quite pretty. Of course, you have seen newspaper charts of all of these. We took Iheya without opposition. There had been some Japanese there, but they apparently considered defense impracticable and went to Okinawa in boats after the shooting began on Okinawa. Some of them probably got through. There is much disease and malnutrition among the natives on Iheya. Aguni lies off to the west of the Hagushi area of Okinawa, where the original landings were made. It has a fairly nice cliff on one end, but is otherwise undistinguished." (Adams, 2002) Radar and fighter direction centers had been established on the islands. 791 arrived on the 14th and loaded the LVT's of Company A 726th Amphibious Tractor Battalion, Ships Platoon E and Military Government Detachment B-2 HQ 2nd Marine Division. They arrived on the 15th and anchored off Naha Harbor, there they disembarked Ships Platoon E U.S.M.C. They got underway for Aguni Shima on the 17th and arrived the same day. There they disembarked the LVT and personnel of Company A 726 Amphibious Tractor Battalion and the Military Government Detachment H.Q. of the 2nd Marine Division. After going to G.Q. they made preparations on the 18th for returning to Okinawa and anchored in berth How. They passed the Okinawa capital city a Naha as it lay in ruins, staying until the 20th of June and began preparations to get underway for Leyte. MoMM1c C. W. Keck reported back aboard from being hospitalized at the U. S. Naval Hospital on Saipan.

LST 791 left for Leyte on June 22 and arrived June 27 at San Pedro Bay. They had been the fourth ship outboard at the berth 46. LST 557 moored alongside to starboard, with AD-34, USS Alcor [a repair ship], and PCS-1421 [Patrol Craft] moored alongside to port. Patrol craft of the 1376 class had been 136 feet long and armed with one 3inch gun, one 40 mm AAA gun and two 20 mm guns. They worked topside and got paid. Weaver noted on the 29th that he had been supposed to get paid $172.96 the next day. That day he signed the pay receipt but hadn't received it yet. On 2nd of July they received some supplies. July 2 General Joseph Stilwell, General Buckner's replacement, announced that Okinawa was secure and that campaign was officially over. The ship's canteen got resupplied on the 4th and the second section got liberty. On the 6th the ship received gasoline and fuel oil, but the weather had become socked in all afternoon limiting maneuvers. The following men reported aboard for duty M. D. Rowland WT3c, V. V. Velvendy AS(R), Jack M. Neugebauer AS(R), D. M. Omlin AS(R), Howard J. Lang F2c, Elver L. Lankins AS(R), Patrick O'Malley AS, William G. Pryor AS(R), and Hubert Farrow S2c. On the 8th the following departed the vessel for Coast Guard-Army Manning Detail and transportation to the states: Merle S. Wilson G.Q.M, Gilbert Smith Jr. S1c, and Leon Motola S1c. At 1304 hours on the 8th they left for Cebu and arrived at Magellan Bay there at 1707 hours on the 9th. The crew knew they had three weeks of maneuvers coming up.

They maneuvered off Danao Point Cebu on the 10th with Weaver drilling in the rubber boat all day and the next. On the 12th they prepared to receive military casualties through the bow in the target area. 791 anchored in Cebu Harbor on the evening of the 14th. July 15th the first section got liberty. They left for the old anchorage on the 16th. A new engine was installed in small boat #2 on the 17th. The 18th saw them again drilling with the rubber boat. The 19th saw Assistant Surgeon Jack Wilson U.S.P.H.S.R. report aboard for duty. Twentieth of the month saw them resume drills with Lt. (jg) R.C. Ball USNR and a medical party from the APA-161 U.S.S. Dickens [attack transport] aboard. Assistant Surgeon John H. Pritchett Jr. USPH was transferred to the LST-559 for further transportation as was John W.

Papsun PhoM3c. They drilled with medical party from USS Dickens. On the 23rd they set sail for Luzon and on that same day the American flag was raised on the southern tip of Okinawa. The 791 arrived at Tayabas Bay, Luzon on the 24th at 1307 hours. The 25 was a special day the crew got liberty in the city of Luzon. Commander Roughton USN, Commander Anderson USCG and Lt. Commander McNevitt USNR came aboard from APA-208, USS Talladega [attack transport] and they got underway exercising at beaching off Abung, Tayabas Bay Luzon. They left by small boat at 1525 hours finishing the exercise. On the 30 they moored to the starboard side of LST 559 and commenced loading commissary supplies. On the 31st they shifted ballast to give a 5 degree list to facilitate painting of the hull. They also started getting ill sailors for treatment and then transferring them back afterwards.

United States Public Health Service corps had been militarized during the war. It provided medical officers primarily to the Coast Guard. Militarization can be done by an act of congress or by executive order. Uniforms and ranks are identical to the U. S. Navy and Coast Guard.

Further History Of Doctors As They Come And Go

Do you recall my telling you about Dr. Pritchett, who turned up in April after setting out in November? And that the day he turned up his orders came to return to the States upon being relieved? That was 17 April (the orders were dated 12 May) Cluxton was ordered out to relieve him.

Well, I didn't tell Dr. Pritchett for about a month, anticipating what actually happened, because he was supposed to start flight surgeon's school on 22 April or as soon thereafter as he could get back after being relieved, and I knew he would be disappointed. In May I told him, but cautioned him not to write his wife unless he wanted to take a chance on disappointing her. He wrote her anyway (he is only 24) and two days later we learned that Dr.

Cluxton had hotfooted it to Washington and gotten his orders changed, a second McNulty. Of course Dr. Pritchett was crushed, and didn't know what to tell his wife, either. so he stewed around at a terrific rate for two months, saying "what do you think I should t e l l my wife?" to anyone who would listen. About two weeks ago he finally quit stalling and told her it was all a mistake and he wasn't coming home. But a relief was finally dug up for him and arrived several days ago. We have packed the Doc off in a state of justifiable confusion. We had a lot of fun out of Dr. Pritchett because he once told Mr. Bohrer he (B.) had an abnormal startle reaction. A couple of days later we were in Kerama Retto and got underway at first light to discharge some cargo. We had to cross a seaplane runway and at about six o'clock a twin-engined plane took off right astern of the ship very low. The motors made a good deep roar. The Doc thought it was one of the Japs coming aboard the hard way and got out of his bunk, rushed to the head, and flung himself on the deck, a bare and quivering mass. Mr. Bohrer came in to shave at that point and as a consequence the subject of startle reactions was thoroughly discussed for several days to come. The new Doctor is named Wilson and is from Texas. He is quiet, a virtue in a shipmate, and any idiosyncrasies will be faithfully recorded for your amusement.

Things I'll Never Understand

When I was a young man and all fired up with intellectual curiosity either I understood something that came into my sphere of activity or I belabored the subject, and myself, in an effort to find the answers. In those days I either did not know or would not admit that there were any questions too difficult for an answer.

But now that I am old and sage, I realize and confess that there are a good many things which will never be comprehended by anyone. We may guess, but not know. So when the war began I opened up a special department in my *mind entitled THINGS TILL NEVER UNDERSTAND, feeling certain that my naval career would amplify my realization of what I know not.*

This device has been very useful indeed. Many of my associates, envying my calm when the orders conflict, the signals make no sense, or a mild administrative muddle raises its head, have established a similar device to their profit.

One thing in particular I am convinced I know nothing about is why our enemies act the way they do. This is no great loss; the deficiency can be made up by a careful reading of Madeleine's history books, most of which will probably be written by conscientious objectors. Or the ATLANTIC MONTHLY or even READERS DIGEST may favor us with a five-page button-up of the Fascist mind. Of course one gets a differing perspective through a peep- sight than when viewing the enemy from the summits of Radio City. The latter view is undoubtedly more objective and detached. In fact, it is so detached that it probably never heard of a couple of incidents which I am about to drag out of my intellectual skeleton closet.

Read me the answer to this: On D-day the Japs apparently thought we were going to land on the southern part of the island, whereas we landed on the western beaches. They concentrated their defensive units in the south. This was a simple mistake. But within a thousand or so yards of our beaches were two of the best airfields in the Ryukyu's. They were protected by many guns and other installations. These weren't manned. Even that, though incautious, is explicable. But when our people moved in there was literally almost no one there. I heard there was one man on one airfield, a few on the other. Where were the maintenance personnel? They could have fought from the pillboxes there. They were not needed for the southern defense sector since they were not combat troops. The fields were under attack, but they were not unusable. Had we been delayed there our air power would have been that much longer getting established. They say it was quite an odd feeling, to move into those deserted areas. (Since writing that I have learned more about how many Japs were on the island, and their failure to defend the airfields is even more mystifying.)

Here is another odd one: On D plus 1 or D, plus 2 the Japs knew we had their airfields, but all the same a plane deliberately came into one. It was a single-engined fighter plane with plenty of gas and ammunition. He strafed an LVT, setting it on fire, circled the field, and calmly landed. Our people stopped firing and covered him. The pilot got out, put his head down, and started running toward nowhere in particular. He was shot. The next day a fighter plane came in, strafed a pillbox, and landed. The pilot ran and was shot. Nobody here seems able to figure that out. Were the pilots saki'd up? Were they indulging in the Japanese gesture of contempt accomplished by committing hari-kari on an enemy's doorstep? You guess; I just work here.

24 June 1945

Several times I have watched Jap planes in the rays of searchlights. The first time the character up in the sky just cruised along looking around. A twin-engine bomber. He went right over the transport area with all the large caliber guns in the place blazing away at him, and when he got almost out of searchlight range obligingly turned around and came back. He was quite high, but within range. He took no evasive action at all. The shooting was pretty bad; he went home. As far as we know he never did drop any bombs. What impressed us was the way he just streamed along in a straight line. Any self-respecting German pilot would have been cavorting all over the place. Another Jap tried the same thing sometime later and took a slug. He put the nose right down so as to get where he was going in a hurry. About half way down there was an explosion and he shed a few pieces. The plane fell harmlessly in the water. If he was aiming for someone guess the explosion threw him off the target. But the question is, why don't they take evasive action.

Remember the Sunday you said you hoped I wasn't at Okinawa? Well, I was, but it was quiet on the whole. That day a lone Jap kept popping in and out of a cloud over the beach. Maybe he was sending a story home about us, maybe he was trying to make up his mind. He wasn't really inexplicable, but he was an odd number. He was knocked down without having a chance to explain his intentions.

For all these tidbits about the Japs, I would rather fight them than the Germans. There has been a good deal of air activity, but they are expending an awful lot of planes and of course they have many more naval targets in this theater. There is no use calling attention to Jap deficiencies, but the Germans were more effective, plane for plane. When the war is over we'll be glad to point out the Japs' mistakes.

On July 4th the commanding officer wrote a letter to the crew. It read:

U.S.S. LST-791
Fleet Post Office
San Francisco, Calif.
4 July 1945
From: Commanding Officer

To: each crewman had his name in this space

1. Because memory is short and because recognition of your combat duty should be assured, this is written by a grateful commanding officer to serve as a permanent record of your participation in the Okinawa campaign. It will certify that as a member of the ship's company of LST 791 you carried United States Marines from Guadalcanal to Ulithi to Okinawa, participating in the major assault on April 1, 1945. It will remind you of the useful and varied load we carried through rough seas; LVTs, pontoon causeways, and LCT, gasoline, ammunition, field rations, and other odds and ends which serve the forces of invasion. This will establish the fact that you stayed at the beachhead throughout the period of 1-11 April 1945, defending your ship and cargo

effectively against the attacks of the enemy and delivering the goods intact.

2. On your return to the Marianas, after availability, the ship took on a full load of Army ammunition. With a small tug in tow you returned to Okinawa, arriving on 19 May. After unloading the ammunition and dispatching the tug, you performed varied duties at Okinawa, Ie Shima, Kerama Retto, Iheya, and Aguni, leaving the area on 22 June. This was the day Okinawa was declared secured.

3. The large number of Marines and other passengers carried to Okinawa taxed the ship's facilities and presented many problems. Your successful handling of these is affirmed by the enclosed letter from the Marine commanding officer, Lt. Colonel H. C. Woodhouse Jr.

4. Your fine work in this campaign has made you and your ship a tempered weapon, ready for further use against the enemies of your country.

Passed by Naval Censor
(s) WBN
Andrew Duncan Jr.
Lieutenant, USCGR.
NOT FOR PUBLICATION OR BROADCAST BY RADIO

PRACTICING FOR INVASION OF JAPAN

◇◇◇◇◇◇

August 1 in the early morning several feet of water was discovered in the port shaft alley. The cause was determined to be a high pressure fire main being allowed to pass through the shaft alley suction valves. Number 1 and 2 fresh water pump motors had been put out of commission. Machinery spare parts were wet and needed to be rewrapped. August 2, the crew awakened at 0630 hours for anchor practice maneuver. They got paid that day and Weaver got $59.00. As a bonus also there had mail call. On the 3rd Weaver got up at 0500 hours for anchor detail at 0800 hours. They received 38,872 gallons of diesel oil from LST 972 after finishing maneuvers that day. For the next several days they practiced maneuvers as before. They practiced with medical parties from APA-211, U.S.S. Missoula [attack transport]. Some of the crew started to speculate that they had been practicing for another invasion. They had been and the target was to be the home islands of Japan. It was to be the largest invasion in history. According to intelligence it was going to be bloody from all the tricks plus a few more the Japanese had learned to use up to this point in the war. It was to be called Operation Olympic and had been scheduled for November 1, 1945. Casualties had been estimated to be a million.

However, during rehearsing for the invasion, Hiroshima had been hit by the first atomic bomb ever used in war on August 6, it was called Little Boy. On the 9th Russia declared war on Japan and the same day Nagasaki had been hit by the second atomic bomb, Fat Man. The crew had not been aware of the atomic bombs having been dropped. It wasn't until they had been underway to Tokyo for occupation duty that the skipper informed the crew of the atomic bomb attacks. August 14 the crew was watching a movie, "A Tree Grows in Brooklyn", when the duty officer, Lt. Adams, sounded out "Now hear this, the war is over, the Japs have surrendered." (Adams, 2002) The crew jumped up and cheered, hugged each other and then sat down to watch the end of the movie. When the movie ended then the celebrations begun, grapefruit juice mixed with alcohol; from a prior supply trip made by Lt. Adams himself. They had been thankful for the course of events with the atomic bombings, meant that they didn't have to invade Japan. It had been reported that there seemed to be a lot of hangovers the next morning. Weaver speculated that he should be home in about 6 months.

Hirohito

By the Grace of Heaven, Emperor of Japan, seated on the Throne occupied by the same Dynasty changeless through ages eternal, to all to whom these Presents shall come, Greeting!

He do hereby authorize Mamory Shigenitsu, Zyosarat, First Class of the Imperial Order of the Rising Sun to attach his signature by command and in behalf of Ourselves and Our Government unto the Instrument of Surrender which is required by the Supreme Commander for the Allied Powers to be signed.

In witness whereof, We have hereunto set Our signature and caused the Great Seal of the Empire to be affixed. Given at Our Palace In Tokyo, this first day of the ninth month of the twentieth year of syowa, being the two thousand six hundred and fifth year from the Accession of the Emperor Zinmu.

Seal of the
Signed: HIROHITO
Countersigned: Naruhiko-o Prime minister

PROCLAMATION

Accepting the terms set forth in Declaration Issued by the= heads of the Governments of the United States, Great Britain and China on July 26th, 1945 at Potsdam and subsequently adhered to by the Union of Soviet Socialist Republics, We have commanded the Japanese Imperial Government and the Japanese Imperial General Headquarters to sign on Our behalf the Instrument of Surrender presented by the Supreme Commander for the Allied Powers and to issue General Orders to the Military and Naval Forces In accordance with the direction of the Supreme Commander for the Allied Powers. We command all Jur people forthwith to cease hostilities, to lay down their arms and faithfully to carry out all the provisions of Instrument of Surrender and the General Orders issued by the Japanese Imperial Government and the Japanese Imperial General Headquarters hereunder.

This second day of the ninth month of the twentieth year of Syowa.

Seal of the Signed HIROHITO
Manoru Shigenitau Ministerf or Poreigo Affairs
Iwao Yamazaki Minister for Home Affairs
Juichi Toushima Minister of Finance
Sadany Shimonura Minister of War
Mitsunasa Yonal Winiater of Navy

Chuzo Iwata Minister of Justice

Tamon Haeda Minister of Education

Kenzo Matsuura Minister of Welfare

Kotaro Sengoku Ministero of Agriculture and Forestry

Chikuhe1 Nakajina Minister of Commerce and Industry

Maoto Kobiyama Minister of Transportation

Junisaro Ionos Ministor without Portofollo

Taketora Ogata Miniaterwithout Portofollo

Binahiro Obata Minister without Portof011o

Emperor

Countersigned: Maruhiko-8

Prime Minister

Signed at TOKYO BAY .JAPAN

SECOND -d a y of.... September, 1945.

On the 15th of August they got underway for Subic Bay at 1903 hours. For the first time they had a show on the main weather deck. They arrived in Subic Bay at 1000 hours on the 16th. August 18th they moored alongside AOG-20, USS Seekonk [fleet gasoline tanker] and took on 56,131 gallons of diesel oil. They also received 810 gallons of lube oil from the naval supply base. On the 25th they departed and arrived in Manila on the 25th at 1910 hours. On the 26 they unloaded oil drums from the main deck. There, they also loaded on the 27th Company D, E and F 1303 General Service Combat Army Engineers fresh from Europe. These troops landed in Normandy on D-Day and had been a part of General Patton's 3rd Army, VIII Corps seeing action in northern Europe, Battle of the Bulge, Rhineland and central Europe. Some of the crew recalled them to be "mad as hell", (Riley, 1943-1945) while others remembered their spirit to be good, except for some "routine beefing". (Riley, 1943-1945) In Manila they got liberty. The city noted by one crewman looked to be nearly destroyed. On the 29 they saw M. Baker MoMM3c, B. L. Bryant GM1c, R. L. Anderson CBM, R. E. Burdick GM1c, C. J. Donnelly CGM, G. W. Frank S1c and R. F. Schlernitzauer BM1c depart the ship for transport back to the states for discharge. J. E. Morley PhM2c was transferred to the Naval Dispensary in Manila for treatment. August 31, General McArthur landed at Atsugi airport in Japan and proceeded to drive himself to Yokohama.

Manila

My observation of Manila was of limited scope and duration, but some things stood out quite clearly.

Like many large cities, Manila is composed of several smaller cities all contiguous but all distinguishable. The demarcations, though slightly blurred by the damage, are clearer than in many cities. The Chinese section is very distinctive; the poor suburbs approach in places the wretched hovels of the rural sections. The metropolitan section contains some very substantial old structures, including the inevitable cathedrals, which maybe relics of the Spanish era. There is an old-fashioned business district with office buildings of the type built in the early twenties in the midst of less pretentious structures, such as grocery stores. It is a sort of cross between Mobile, Market street, and parts of Oran. The entrepreneur's proprietary interest in the sidewalk, one of the more valuable intangible assets of any business conducted by those of Latin blood or background, is clearly manifested in this section.

Then there is the part of town which was planned, and which as a consequence has broad streets, traffic circles, large public buildings, and vacant places where further luster was intended for the Pearl of the Orient. A few buildings are relatively intact, but most of them are gutted, dynamited, or at least shot up. In some of the poorer sections damage was haphazard and limited, but a good many of the better buildings were ruined. The overall destruction is not comparable to that of a city which has been carefully bombed and subjected to artillery attack, such as Bizerte. But is bad enough, and it was the result of vandalism, not war.

Miscellaneous Observations Of An Army Engineer. July 27, 1945

One day an Army Engineer was aboard for a while. He had served in China for a while and had helped build some of the Chinese air bases. He said it was quite amazing what the Chinese had done in the way of building air strips and roads by hand. They are just like ants, apparently. He had seen children building roads by carrying earth on large leaves. In time they get them built. Apparently the reason they don't all burn out from this labor is the fact that haste is not considered essential. There are frequent conferences for this and that, and meals, while not ample, are frequent. The Chinese evidently take a few Jap prisoners. When one of these is marched by all thousand of the human ants will rush over and shout insults quite bravely, returning to their labors in due time. Of course all this is hearsay, but the Chinese and their upart of the war do sound quite interesting. Even as the bulldozer is our Engineers' favorite weapon, the steamroller is the Japs'. They will try to take them anywhere and over the most difficult, with fair success. The earth they tamp down is carried by hand, by impressed labor.

When this Engineer officer left China he went to the Philippines. He says he ran into some guerillas at a place where the Japs had been particularly brutal and they had caught a Jap soldier. They made him eat his ears then cut his head off. The Engineer got in late, but said he felt the guerrillas had overdone themselves a bit.

OCCUPATION DUTY

On the first of September they made preparations for heavy weather at 1945 hours. September 2, 1945 V.J. Day, LST 791 still in Manila harbor. The ship left at 1620 hours on the 3rd for Tokyo Bay. Weaver noted in his diary on the 10th that he had 40 points, therefore he hoped to get discharged soon. Military authorities had a point system for being shipped states side. The point system based on length of service, time overseas, wounds, medals, and number of children under 18 years old in the family. Initially seven crewmen had qualified for early departure and only had to wait for that opportunity in Japan.

Bad Weather Of 18 September 1945

The course of the typhoon was reported from time to time, as is customary. One over-excited report of 17 September gave an estimated 135-knot wind velocity to be anticipated for the Tokyo area.

The next report said no danger was expected in the Tokyo. We turned in with no crystallized anticipations, but when the barometer fell from 29.73 at 2000 to 29.56 at 2400 we gathered that something unpleasant might be expected. By 0130 it was blowing handily, so I had the main engines warmed up. At 0400, the wind having increased steadily, we commenced steaming to the anchor with 1/3 on one engine. We had 100 fms. of chain out, our whole scope, in 17 fms. of water.

The barometer was 29.36. We increased engine speed as the wind built up, finally running both engines at 160 RPM (125 being 1/2, 180 2/3).

Many of the ships were dragging and one set by us about 0400 onto a ship astern, their anchor chains becoming fouled. Separation was ultimately accomplished. As the anchorage was in the open bay there was a strong tendency to drag. However, the shallowness of the water reduced the size of the seas.

When visibility became good between squalls, about 0515, it became clear that a Navy freight and passenger ship had dragged into our anchorage and was about a mile ahead of us. She attempted to pick up her anchor and maneuver clear, but was set down very fast while attempting to run across the wind. Bud Leake's ship was on our starboard bow, another LST on our port bow. The AK (auxiliary cargo) ran across Bud's anchor chain, parting it, then hit his bow, not too hard. He then ran across the other ship's bow hard, parting his chain, doing general damage forward and opening a bow door. The latter Ship was the closer to us. For some reason his engines were not going so we used our limited maneuvering power to go to starboard. After he had cleared, we went to port and Bud's ship cleared. It had power about the time it came abeam, and may have had it earlier. The other ship had no power and laid herself across the bow of an IST astern of us, doing some damage to herself at about frame 12 and vicinity. Small boats left in the water were breaking loose. Some sank. None came very close. Only two that I heard of had personnel in them. Do not know what happened to these boats. If they were able to keep the pumps going, they were probably able to ride it until they fetched up. At 0845 the following message was received:

"Revised weather forecast. Typhoon center expected to pass over or fairly close to this station about181800 I. Winds should increase steadily to s.s.E. 60 knots with gusts up to 80 knots close to center. After passage of center wind will

shift to N.W. 60 knots gusting to 88 knots. Winds will then decrease to N.W. 40 knots by 182400 I. 6 to 10 foot rise in water level expected after peak wind velocities. Mountainous swells from S.W. will occur outside harbor entrance. Waves in unprotected harbor areas expected to reach 15 feet."

Mr. Horton and I were inclined to doubt the time of 1800 and thought the center would pass north, having been studying our data on the subject avidly. However, we took the necessary extreme measures indicated and dutifully passed the word on to the crew. We were under orders to sail at 1030 and of course laughed around at a great rate about our preparations to sail. The orders were finally cancelled.

At 1000 the barometer reached a low of 29.25, holding it until after 1100. By 1200 it was up a hundredth, and held until 1400, when i t registered 29.30. The wind started easing a t about 1500 and by 1630 it was no longer necessary to steam to the anchor.

The sun set on a calm sea. We asked the C.T.U. for the wind velocity and received the following answer. (His ship was alongside a dock.) Visual Dispatch. Action Adee LST 791.

From: (Originator) CTF 33. Heading: DWorf 791 V. Dovecote 25 181336. wind velocity is this shelter dock area are not representative of exposed harbor areas highest record is 40 knots gusts to 60 knots 181800/I Intend check records of other ships outside breakwater for their data Will forward data when obtained BT 181336.

Both Bud Leake's ship and the other one are in convoy with us now.

The door of the other one is very much askew but they have it secured somehow and are plowing right along. I think they deserve a lot of credit.

On the 11th still underway for Tokyo they watched movie topside. Before arriving at 1303 hours on the 12th the reversing mechanism on the port main engine failed to function properly, requiring that engine to be secured. They arrived in Yokohama Anchorage Tokyo Bay on the starboard engine at 1325 hours. The skipper, Lieutenant Duncan recalled that the bay was protected by two extensive breakwaters. Cranes and railways enabled extensive heavy cargo to be handled. Industrial plants lined the waterfront just behind the docks. Most of the industrial facilities standing still, some burned out, some slightly damaged and some untouched. However, the business and residential section had been almost demolished, except for some isolated buildings, the rest was flattened. LST 791 has the distinction of being the first ship larger than a minesweeper to enter Tokyo harbor after peace was made. The harbor is at the head of the bay, several miles from Yokohama. They had to navigate a fairly narrow channel one afternoon, just as the Army found out that the concrete ramp that they selected had no way out for mechanized equipment the ship carried. They went up river and found no suitable place to unload. After that they went back to the ship and then to Yokohama to unload.

Tokyo

The LST 791 had the distinction of being the first ship larger than a minesweeper to enter Tokyo Harbor after the peace. And it will probably continue to be the only LST ever to enter.

Tokyo Harbor is at the head of Tokyo Bay, several miles above Yokahama. Entry is made by a fairly narrow channel. The harbor itself is long and is wide enough for easy maneuvering. Facilities are good but not as extensively developed as Yokahama's.

We went in one afternoon and arrived inside just as the Army discovered that the concrete ramp they had selected for us had no egress for the mechanized equipment we carried. So we tied up to a mooring buoy and Mr. Horton, Major Graddison, and myself went ashore for a reconnaissance. We proceeded quite far up the river, but there was no suitable place to discharge the load. The only result of that search and the similar one the next morning was some good sight-seeing. We ultimately had to go back to Yokahama and discharge our cargo there, though the Army would have preferred Tokyo had a suitable *beach been found. The other LST's booked for Tokyo did not even enter the harbor and all LST unloading scheduled for Tokyo was transferred to Yokahama.*

Just as we were about to moor in the harbor, having managed the channel by constant use of the sounding lead and a liberal application of luck, what should come puffing up but a Japanese pilot boat and an important-looking pilot. The Jacobs Ladder was over the side for the use of the beachmaster, so it was hauled up just as the pilot hove alongside. While I was unable to see him from the conn it is reported that he was suffering great loss of face and was requesting that the ladder be lowered. It was not, and I fear it is barely possible that some unruly members of the crew may have been unnecessarily emphatic in advising the pilot that having entered the harbor without his assistance we would be able to tie up to the buoy unaided. We much regretted that we were unable to go into the interior of the city, which, like that of Yokahama, is reported to be largely destroyed. Some portions of the business and shopping sections are reported in good condition, though and I would like to have gotten some gifts. Near the waterfront there was little destruction. A few warehouses had been burned. Most of the people had been moved away from the waterfront and the impression was almost that of a deserted city. A few people were fishing from the docks. No chimneys were smoking, no vehicles were visible. There were signs of looting and a few Japs were seen quietly engaging in this time-honored Oriental practice when we went up the river we passed under a fine-looking 3-span cantilever bridge with white stone supports. The middle span was navigational; a draw bridge with the cantilever under the roadway, bisected rather than hinged at only one end. As it was dusk, we felt ourselves lucky not to get a fishhook in the eye from the anglers above, if nothing worse.

A ferry which passed ahead of us showed that there was still life in the somnolent city; it was crowded and reminded us a little of--well, there. Is a ferry in Dartmouth like it, but the English would resent the likeness. The occasion gave rise to much mutual rubber-necking. We were in an LCVP, which I'll grant is odd looking anyway, and it must have been the first American boat to come above the bridge. A number of Japs waved, but we maintained a glum and conquering impassivity.

From the sea, most cities look alike in so many respects that the differences are easier to remark than the similarities. And now that I think of the appearance of the Tokyo waterfront I realize that most of the notable details are so purely nautical as to be of little significance to one who has not spent a good deal of time looking at cities waterfront first. However, one thing which had a fairly distinct character was a poor part of the city where it impinged upon the river. It was crowded, as all poor parts are, but worse, and even in the soft light of evening there was something evil and diseased about the Flimsy mass. The stilted structures tottering above the water made me think of a glacier, as if the sinister things evolving there were from time to time cast out into the world.

Yokohama–Saipan 7 November 1945

791 had been about to tie up, after navigating the channel by constant use of sounding lead and a liberal application of luck, when a Japanese boat came up alongside with an important appearing person, the pilot. Jacob's ladder already over the side for the use of the beach master had been hauled up as the pilot boat came alongside. The Japanese pilot having suffered a great loss of face requested the ladder be lowered. It had not. Skipper feared that some of the more unruly members of the crew may have been unnecessarily emphatic in addressing the pilot that they had entered the harbor without his assistance and would not need his assistance in tying up. The ship beached in Yokohama on the 14th at 19:30 hours to unload the cargo. Soldiers then cleaned the ship for the crew. At 0630 hours on 15th Company D, E, and F of the 1303 Engineers left.

The People We Took To Tokyo

In June of 1943, when I was getting ready for an excursion to Sicily and people at a safe distance were still talking about the soft underbelly of Europe, the 1303d Engineers arrived in England. To give you an idea of how the service was mushrooming in those days, it was the 36th Engineers we took to Licata; they had come to Africa with the great old 3d Division. So the 1303d were probably pretty green when they got to England.

During the next year they must have learned a great deal, because when they landed in Normandy on the greatest D-day of the war they evidently gave a pretty good account of themselves. Then they followed General Patton's wild-riding 3d Army right across Europe. They worked hard, were in five major battles, and saw the whole show.

In July of this year they went to Marseilles and embarked for Manila. The only pause was at the Panama Canal, where they awaited their turn like every one does. In August they reached Manila, which is not a garden spot. Early the next month they came aboard us to go to Tokyo.

Some of them became eligible for point discharge while we were enroute. Maybe they will get home in a few months.

Their spirit is good. Except for a little routine beefing, they do not crab. They did not expect the war to be a picnic and it isn't. They are good soldiers; we were proud to have them aboard and we told them so.

Captain Duffield. 9 November 1945

On our last run to Japan we carried very nice guy named Captain Duffield, who had a fine artillery outfit that had fought on Saipan, Leyte and Okinawa. The details of this story may be a little hazy, but in essence it is as he told it to me several weeks ago. A lucky Jap shell hit the Battery's ammunition dump on Okinawa and a first-rate series of explosions began. One of Captain Duffield's men saw that fire had reached his pup tent and crawled out from cover to get

132

a picture in the pup tent before it was destroyed. (We are running fast and vibrating badly, hence the wavy writing.) An explosion at this point caught the lad with a shell fragment in the leg. He was sent back to a field hospital and from there Captain Duffield learned that he was sent to a hospital ship. That was toward the end of the campaign. Several weeks later, when things quieted down, Captain Duffield got a formal notification that Coker (that was the man's name) had died. Normally he would have written Coker's next of kin. But he didn't believe Coker was dead. Captain Duffield fills the average man's conception of a Texan. He is very large, speaks softly and slowly, is courteous, thoughtful, and calm. He is a fine friend and the fact that he has eliminated several Japs personally disinclines me to select him as a desirable enemy. He is a reasonable and somewhat reflective man, and for this reason is hard to sway when his mind is made up. His mind was made up that Coker had not died. "Hell," he told me, "He might have lost the leg but it just didn't stand to reason that the man would die." He certainly wasn't going to disturb Coker's family by telling them Coker was dead. It just didn't stand to reason well, it was his duty to write a letter. People were beginning to make a fuss about it. So he doubled himself up at the hinges and got into a jeep and went to Regimental Headquarters. They said the man was dead all right. The War Department had sent his family a telegram. Captain Duffield should write. So he reflected upon the matter and went to the Graves Registration Service. They had Coker, all right. Brought ashore from the hospital ship with another man. The records showed they were buried together, in adjoining graves, 18 days or two weeks before. Had he written Coker's family? Captain Duffield considered the matter anew and returned to Regimental Headquarters. An order for exhumation was what he wanted. Of course it was pointed out to him that he was taking up a lot of everybody's time, including his own, and that a letter should be written to Coker's family. He patiently and in his soft voice averred that it just didn't stand to reason that Coker had died. So they gave him the order. The little party was assembled for the mournful task, and two of the man's closest associates went along for identification. The grave

133

was located by an annoyed representative of the Graves Registration Service and the digging commenced. At about the right depth the spades touched something solid and uncovered a blanket. The Chaplain drew nearer and the exhumation proceeded. The blanket was uncovered. Carefully it was folded back. There was Coker's leg. Captain Duffield then considered it appropriate to write a letter to Coker's family. He apologized for any mental anguish or distress the War Department's telegram had caused. He said it didn't stand to reason Coker could have died. But he was sorry about the leg. The family wasn't worried, though. Coker had been flown back to the States and was sent home for convalescence. He had opened the telegram.

Yokohama

Tokyo Bay is one of the finest bays in the world and Yokohama is a great industrial port which takes full advantage of its position on the Bay. It is protected by two extensive breakwaters and has good dock space. Inlets enlarge the alongside area and it is apparent from the soundings we were getting that the bottom has been dredged out to a greater depth than that shown on the charts. Hammerhead cranes and railway facilities enable bulky lifts to be handled without great difficulty. Extensive industrial plants of all sorts line the waterfront just back of the docks.

Behind the industrial section was apparently the business and residential section. Most of the industrial plants are standing. Some are burned out, some are slightly damaged, some untouched. Damage here was disappointing. But the business and residential section was practically demolished. Some isolated buildings stood, a few shells, and the rest was a flattened waste. The rubble was of a flimsy light type and in many places the construction must have been of such a type that it was almost all consumed by fire. What remained of their architecture was. undistinguished by any remarkable features. It was an imitation of conventional European and American including some of the less desirable modernistic.

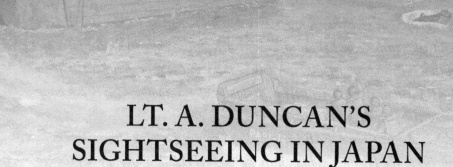

LT. A. DUNCAN'S SIGHTSEEING IN JAPAN

6 Sept 1945

The Bronze Buddha Of Kamakura

The bronze buddha of Kamakura is easily the most impressive single thing I have viewed in Japan. The four little photographs were purchased at the site. I am completely unable to identify the objects in the three small photographs not of the Buddha. Though I did not remain long in silent communion with this bronze idol, I consider the interview very enlightening. The idol spends his time in passive contemplation of those who are energetic and curious enough to come and gaze at him. Since he-keeps his great big mouth permanently shut, his reputation as a prophet is never diminished by a mistake and no one ever goes away disappointed.

At the gates to the grounds the following sign appears "Stranger, whosoever be thy gods or whatsoever be thy creed, remember as you enter here that the ground you tread has been hallowed by the worship of the Ages."

The Buddha was cast in sections (the seams are horizontal and just visible in the photographs.) A temple was erected around it many years ago, but a tidal wave has since destroyed sections (the seams are horizontal the temple and is said to have moved the statue 30 feet.

November 10 1945

FA FA'S Visit. (FA FA is a term of endearment by his daughters)

Draw up your high chairs, my frowsy-headed l i t t l e darlings, and FAFA will tell you how he happened to visit a Japanese household. The facts are rather involved, and if you can follow them you will be doing better than FAFA will do when he is as old as the square of your combined ages; but hang on to your jello cups and away we'll go.

In the first place, FAFA is a well-known sucker for kiddies. This even applies to the Japanese kiddies if they give FAFA half a break, even though the old boy was earnestly trying to score on the Japs just a few months

Well, I was standing in this little shop in Hakkodate one morning scowling angrily at other customers who came in and out leaving the door open to the wintry blast, when who should come tripping in on their tiny get but two of the cutest little girls in the Japanese Empire. And they were just the ages of you, Mammy-Pie, and you, my darling little Weezie what doesn't even know her own FAFA. This even applies to the Japanese kiddies if they give FAFA half a break, even though the old boy was earnestly trying to score on the Japs just a few months back. Now I am not a great fraternizer with the Japs, for reasons of no interest to you innocents, but there is no evil in children and certainly these were as appealing as any you would see anywhere. For one thing, they were clean. For another, they were exceptionally well dressed. They were pretty, too; I am beginning to see the differences in Jap facial types. The two little doll-like figures stood there quietly, quite plainly abashed by thus having blundered into the presence of an American soldier. This was unusual; most Japanese children are very forward. Also, all Japanese children's noses run. All but these two noses. In FAFAs complete beguilement he knelled and addressed the children in what he always (and always erroneously) hopes will prove to be a universal language. Why he clings to this oft-shattered illusion is not clear, but you may as well understand it now because if in later life you ever travel with the old boy it may be a source of embarrassment. You will want to learn when to start sidling away and leaving the old codger to his own peculiar methods.

However, the smiles, grimaces, and soft tones in which I expressed myself served as a tenuous bridge over the linguistic gulf, and from the interested and giggling chirps which they exchanged it was evident that they appraised me as a harmless and friendly fool who regretted that he could speak naught but gibberish. Their approbation so bewitched me that I made a great sacrifice. From a pocket (this process was watched with fascination) I dragged a box of candy, my intended lunch, and bestowed a piece upon each of my little friends. They did not grab. At this point the proprietor, who had emerged as the father during my harebrained conversation with the animated dolls, addressed himself to them. In response, the children turned toward me, uttered a few words, and bowed words, bowed, and we all giggled cheerily. They went behind the counter and presently emerged. At the door they turned, said a passable imitation of "Good-bye" and bowed. I glowed and beamed with appreciation, said "Good-bye" and bowed as they rattled away hand in hand.

Later on in the day I was back in the shop and wanted to have something changed. The proprietor indicated that I was to accompany him by the use of signs. This I did, I knew not where. He had only one leg, so our progress was slow. We turned up a narrow street and who should come laughing down it but my two little friends. They had a package for their father, and then I realized for the first time that instead of taking me to another shop where part of the work was farmed out he was taking me home. Presumably Uncle Steve was working away at one of Japan's celebrated home industries.

My prospective host insisted that I come along, because he wanted to make sure everything was all right while we were still in Uncle Steve's neighborhood. (I guess). So I consented and we walked along to an extremely unprepossessing front. Mine host preceded me by a few steps (the kiddies had *already preceded him) and bade me welcome. I paused at the raised platform which is just inside the entrance to Japanese houses, and members of the family were presented. The children had heralded my arrival well, and I was, it seemed to me, being received as a foreign devil who had a distinctly better side. Though I must say to the great credit of the occupation forces that there is very little fear of us.*

There at the threshold a Japanese Social Moment had obviously arrived. I confess that I stalled a bit and smiled a bit longer than necessary to see what they would do. They were Spartan, and did nothing, but it seemed to me obvious as they looked at me that they were thinking will this character have enough sense to take off his shoes?" As I sat down and removed them what I construed as a restrained sigh of relief was barely audible. When we left this spot the man of the house quickly bent over and reversed my shoes so that they pointed outward. I learned later this a mark of respect, a courtesy.

I see it is getting late, my angels. More anon.

More Concerning FAFA'S Visit

At the threshold with the kiddies had been two middle aged women, apparently the mother and Uncle Steve's wife. We proceeded inside; my host having discarded his crutch hopped along much remindful of a rooster, and myself following after him. In the second inner room was an elderly woman kneeling by a brazier and apparently whipping up a l i t t l e tea for lunch. We bowed at each other. The Japanese, by the way, are very practiced bowers. They can bow very gracefully from a sitting, kneeling, or squatting position. I tried this in my cabin one day (privately) and succeeded only in producing an ungracious wrinkle in my ever- thickening mid-portion. I could understand the old lady's interest in the brazier. It was the only visible source of heat. When it gets colder, the Japs simply put on more clothes. The effect must be quite ponderous in sub-zero weather. The braziers burn charcoal or coke. From a heat-producing standpoint they are inefficient;

the radiating surface is very small. We proceeded up a wide flight of steep wooden stairs and I noticed with interest that arranged in tasteful graceful garlands above the stairs were hanging strings of dried small squid, a staple article

Of diet. And the next time, my pampered ones, I hear so much as a squeak out of either of you about your spinach. At the top of the stairs was a passageway or narrow hall with living apartments on each side. We stopped a t the second on the right and the flimsy door was opened by my host. He ushered me in and I preceded him as he apparently desired. There in this little room, sitting with his back to me at a table not over six inches high was - who do you think? - not Hirohito's white horse, not the Bronze Buddha of Kamakura, but Uncle Steve himself. He did not look up from his work and merely uttered a few words.

Our one-legged friend spoke with a rising inflection and Uncle Steve turned his head. Well, he was funny, my sweet ones, and very surprised indeed. Uncle Steve must have been the retiring type and it gave him quite a start to have his immaculate little workshop thus violated. However he grinned nervously and I felt that we were at least potentially en rapport, as your Cousin Ellen is fond of saying. The work done had been satisfactory and after a brief sojourn I departed. The family, even including Grandmother, was mustered to bid me farewell, and the lady of the house presented me with two pears. After demurring briefly, which is said to be proper, I stuffed the pears into the pockets of my parka and bowed. After putting on my shoes, I bowed again. The smaller of my two little charmers made the cutest bow I have ever seen, and I more than ever regretted my lack of the gift of tongues. As I departed I bore away the most wonderful idea. Why not let the children of the world act as its ambassadors, and keep the old people at home where they can't do too much harm. For at the present time it is not the meek that inherit the earth, but the children. Certainly they are the only ones who deserve it.

Sniff, Sniff. 11 November 1945

Every now and then, my tots, you will read some writer's enthusiastic lyric concerning the smell of the salt sea air. Tain't so; the salt marshes have a smell all their own, and the fish around a fishing pier can also be detected from afar; but out in the middle, where the wind can blow for a thousand miles in any direction without seeing anything but the ships that man creates to mock his own smallness, the air has no more smell than fresh water has taste. There are fine heartening smells aboard ship. You should sniff the tarred marline and tarred ratline in my boatswain's locker If you wrinkled up your little button noses (which I suspect you might) I should be greatly disappointed. To me there is no finer aroma than that of tarred small stuff. In a following wind the smell of the baking comes straight to the agonized O.D. During how many first and mid watches have I savored the next day's bread, cakes, or pies, and how appealingly the odor of bacon frying has come into the morning watches. Need I tell you where we went when we came off watch?

Did you ever think of smelling land at sea? Because t h e land in truth has a small, though the sea has not. And how far do you think you would smell it? Well, the reason I thought of this is that we are nearly a day out of Saipan, with some of the lesser islands abeam about 90 miles to windward, and I have just smelled them. How does land smell? Like grass, like trees, like earth . It is not a pungent odor, you understand, but it is distinct. Ninety miles is not so far. If there is a mild steady breeze passing over a large body of land it will hold the land- smell a long time. I have smelled the Azores 200 miles away. But the most peculiar thing I ever noticed of this sort was in 43, when we were approaching the African coast. It was at night; it would be all that night, the next day, the next night and into the following morning before we made a landfall. There was fine warm offshore breeze. There was no one on the bridge but Spika my Polish signalman) and myself. Then with increasing strangeness the smell of land joined us. Well, it was a little eerie. And i t didn't just smell like any land. It smelled like something specific. I feared my imagination was playing tricks on me. One's imagination sometimes becomes a little bit overactive at sea, and we had been 14 days out of sight of land. Spike was a man of independent mind and broad tastes. He had successfully demonstrated his general intelligence as well as his appreciation of music, a bit of verse, and other gifts which life offers to the adventurous male. He could be relied upon. I recall a certain now-it-can-be-told story which has to do with a naval mistake, in the course of which Spika said "By the way, are there as many as six hundred of us?" But I digress.

"What does it remind you of, Spika?" I said. Neither of us had mentioned the smell before. "It is like a circus," he said at once, and I told him that was exactly what had occurred to me. It is odd how things sometimes repeat themselves. Did T tell you that when we were passing through the Tsugaru Straits, between Honshu and Hokkaido, I looked at the water for a while then called the lee helmsman. "Sweeney," sezzi, "Take a look a t the water." He looked. "It's black," he announced. "I never saw it that way before." "Neither did I," I said,

"Except in the Straits of Gibraltar. And I hadn't thought of the incident from that day to this."

On the 16th Lt. (jg) H. T. Durkin, Lt. (jg) R. H. Boher,, F. M. Musser BM2c, C. L. Haight MoMM1c, J. E Price S1c, J. C. Shane MoMM3c, S. C. Waites S1c, L. G. Clark WT3c, G. G. McMahon S2c, R. M. Sullivan Jr. S1c, J. M. Budnick S1c, J. A. Bani Cox, R. F. Weaver S1c, W. J. Yunkin F1c, H. A. Dulemba GM2c, L. M. Suminski S1c, J. W. Dawson S1c, A. J. Finckney CM1c, K. S. McLean QM2c, H. J. Riley Y2c and A. C. Barcewski MoMM2c departed the ship and got berths on the carrier Ticonderoga [CV-14] for a ride back to the states. Those men arrived back in the states on November 5th. The 791 set sail September 19th and arrived back in San Pedro Bay Leyte on the 26 of September. September 27 they moored to YOG-40 [concrete barge used for storage and dispensing diesel oil and gas to ships] and took on 103,908 gallons of diesel oil. Ensign Donald J. Benolken and Lt. Arthur

L. Daughtry reported for duty. Lt. Edward M. Horton was detached from duty with the 791 on the 28. J. E. Schierer MoMM2c, J. T. Bass RM3c, M. E. Stripe S1c, F. O. Angermann SC3c and T. Wershler S1c transferred to replacement pool for transportation stateside the same day. V. J. Dekar FC3c and J. E. Jensen RM3c reported for duty. On the 30th they left and went to Cebu City Harbor arriving on October 1. There they loaded Battery C and service battery of the 306 Field Artillery. This unit was part of the 77th Infantry Division and saw action at Guam, Leyte and Okinawa. They went back to San Pedro and from there to Otaru, Harbor Hokkiado Japan. There they unloaded the troops. Back at Yokohama the dental surgeon Harry A. Kaniss USPHSR reported aboard for duty. At various ports more men had been detached for transport stateside. Fewer reported for duty at those same ports. Going from Yokohama to Saipan and from there to Pearl Harbor they carried troops and equipment. Lt. Edward M. Horton came back aboard on the 4th and took command on 5 December at Pearl, with Lt. Duncan being relieved to go home. Sixth of December saw them set sail for home, after loading 169 servicemen for the trip. The 791 arrived in San Francisco in December 16, 1946 and she was turned over to the Navy. Lt. [jg] Wm. E. Greer USNR assumed command until 27, March 1946. Then Lt. M. E. Katono USCGR commanded the ship until she was decommissioned. The honorable work horse with the Coast Guard crew was decommissioned on the 28th of May 1946. She was struck for the Naval Register on 3, July 1946. The final disposition of the 791 was to be sold to the Walter W. Johnson Co. for scrapping on June 4, 1948.

LST-791 Miscellaneous Statistics

The old girl has now made over a million gallons of fresh water. We took on fresh water at Samar last week, the first time we have received any since 10 May.

We have been out of dry dock over a year. (She had to be hauled out when we got down the river. Water was low and the propellers were bent.)

By the time we get back from Hokkaido I shall have spent every night on the ship for a year, and during that year will have had four meals ashore (1 at San Diego, 1 at Guam, 2 at Pearl).

We have still not gone a alongside a dock in 1945. And oddly enough I have not felt cooped up, because a clean snug ship is so much more desirable than most of the places ashore out here.

The longest straight course we have ever steered was 1500 miles.

Here is a list of the seas I have been in, and right now I hope the list won't get any longer: North, Caribbean, Mediterranean, Tyrrhenian, Irish, Philippine, Bismarck, Solomons, Coral, East China, Mindanao, Camotes, Sulu, South China, Japan.

Beached Oct. 4, 1945 at the Philippines. (Adams, 2002)

*LST 791 going home San Francisco and the
Golden Gate Bridge. (Adams, 2002)*

Going home just outside San Francisco Bay. (Stripe–Bruhn, 2003–2010)

STATESIDE

Max had earned enough points that he got a berth on a troop ship bound for the United States. Upon arriving in San Francisco many of the men celebrated by going out and partying at local establishments, such as the Craby Joes Big Red Barn on 11th and Broadway in Oakland, California with Hillbilly and Cowboy music every night. From San Francisco he took a train to St. Louis, Missouri and discharged from the Coast Guard there. Max then caught another train and returned home Armistice day November 11, 1945 to Omaha, Nebraska at 4:00 am. His wife, Fern, and her folks had been waiting for him at Union Station. He apprenticed as a cement Mason. He help build many buildings and the monument Memorial Park. It was to honor the fallen from the war. It was dedicated by President Harry Truman June 5, 1948. The crew went home to families, jobs, business, careers, schools and other lives. Many stayed in contact over the years. Max Stripe, Robert Weaver and their families stayed in contact and even visited each other. I grew up knowing Weavers family and visiting them, as they visited us. James Morley contacted Fern years later and inquired about Max. A correspondence had been established between them. I remember father stopped in Louisville Kentucky and visited the skipper Andrew Duncan on our way back east for vacation one summer. The skipper being a lawyer had canceled his whole afternoon to speak with and remember the ship and crew with my father. My mother and I stayed in the car and when father came out of his visit with the skipper he showed an exuberance that he rarely showed. It was one of the happiest times; I remember ever seeing for him. Max Stripe died in 1972.

Memorial Park Monument (Omaha NE. 2023)

LIEUTENANT ANDREW W. DUNCAN

The Japs

I supposed that America had demonstrated the possibility of educating the people of any race to be good citizens in a free country. And as a result I have tended to regard peoples for whom I felt no respect with the reserve which the possibility that there but for the Grace of God gives a man. As a result I was somewhat surprised to find that it was impossible for me to look upon the Japs without being aroused to a feeling of actual loathing and contempt. There is something about them that is hardly human, and it is difficult to believe that there is not some profound physiological and mental distinction between them and the other peoples of the world. Distrust is one of the instinctive emotions which they cause. In talking to others who saw them quite casually, as we did, it appeared that these three reactions, aroused in varying degree, were characteristic: dislike, distrust, and are-they- really human. It is difficult to explain these things. I have never seen less truculence in a defeated enemy, or less warmth in the normally friendly American victor. However, there will be so many learned explanations of this curious phenomenon that I shall reserve this matter for the time being and upon my return will drag forth some outdated Sunday supplements for an explanation. (We subscribe to POPULAR SCIENCE MONTHLY, and at Leyte were much edified by one of its issues containing a complete report on the late Special Attack Corps. The author having collected his material in Buffalo, New York, had the benefit of an objective viewpoint which our geographical location had denied us. I must admit that some of his conclusions, though quite obvious to him, had never occurred to us.). Well, at least I can tell you how they look. Have you ever seen a Jap in a soldier's uniform? That's how they look. Four-fifths of the people you see on the streets are soldiers. Many of them seem very young, but it is hard to guess their ages. Many have horn-rimmed glasses. Few are bucktoothed, but there are numerous prominent gold replacements, and, a bizarre touch, some silver ones. When talking to us, even in Japanese, they modulate their voices more softly than when talking to each other. To each other they remind one of parrots and monkeys. Entrepreneurs line what was once Yokohama's main street, with their wares displayed on large open areas provided by the foresight of the United States Army

Air Force. The barest possibility of an impending trade brings a horde of Yokohamans crowding around as though they had been waiting all day to see this particular transaction consummated. They follow the haggling avidly and in their completely metronomic absorption recall the palmier days at Forest Hills.

The most desirable medium of exchange is a pack of cigarettes. There is a method of indicating numbers by fingers, invented by the very young, which bridges many lingual gaps, and which had served me before so that I was able to accomplish a few simple transactions. Having learned in other lands have I told _you I was a world traveler that there is one universally understood American phrase, this was dragged out and used with good effect. The phrase is as follows: "If you think that gismo is worth two packs of cigarettes you're an even bigger dope than you look."

Properly delivered, this utterance is made in an authoritatively *disparaging tone and is followed by a snort, all with feeling. The effect on the listener is to make him utter several short Japanese words after which the trading is resumed as before. As a result of my long experience with international transaction I managed to acquire at least three dollars worth of unadulterated junk for not more than eight dollars cash and one carton of cigarettes.*

Upon taking a general view of the hectic trafficking I had the feeling that I was viewing one of the most peculiar commercial transactions in history; that the victors in the world's greatest war were paying a very adequate reparation to the vanquished. I also had the feeling that had the dealings been conducted by the Jap fleet in the ruins of New York the the feeling that I was viewing one of the most peculiar commercial transactions in history; that the victors in the world's greatest war were paying a very adequate reparation to the vanquished. I also had the feeling that had the dealings been conducted by the Jap fleet in the ruins of New York the prevailing theme would have been much simpler.

THE SKIPPER

Andrew Wallace Duncan, Jr. was born in Greenville, Kentucky on October 12, 1912. His ancestors were from Virginia and Kentucky with strong family, religious and patriotic traits. He graduated from the University of Virginia Law School in 1935 and was practicing law in Louisville, Kentucky when the United States entered World War II. He returned to the home of his relatives in Hampton, Virginia to volunteer for combat duty and was commissioned as a Lieutenant (Junior Grade) in the United States Coast Guard Reserve on June 22, 1942. After extensive training in amphibious warfare he served as a combat commander in both the Atlantic and Pacific, earning battle stars for Morocco, Sicily, Salerno, Okinawa and the Philippines. After the Japanese surrender on September 2, 1945 he commanded the first LST to enter Tokyo Harbor. He was separated as a Lieutenant Commander (USCGR) on February 25, 1946 after extensive combat sea duty in three theaters.

He later practiced law, served as administrative assistant to a United States Senator, and was a counsel in the Department of Defense. He later was founder and chairman of American Child Care Services and

151

the Foundation for the Study of Philanthropy in Hampton, Virginia. He was a director and vice president of the James Monroe Foundation in Fredericksburg, Virginia. He was also an ordained elder in the First Presbyterian Church.

An avid yachtsman, he continued to promote his love of sailing to his extended family. He enjoyed observing the ships of the Atlantic fleet from his home overlooking Hampton Roads. He would share with others, when requested, the exploits of his wartime experiences with his shipmates and the pride he had for their bravery and devotion to duty.

Andrew Wallace Duncan, Jr. died on June 10, 1987 and was buried with his ancestors at St. John's Church in Hampton, Virginia with full military honors rendered by a Coast Guard Honor Guard from Yorktown, Virginia. The legacy he left was that of a patriotic gentleman who deeply loved his family, friends, religion, country and the sea.

DISCOVERY OF
MY FATHERS WAR
EXPERIENCES

I became aware of a LST 791 association and contacted them in 2002. I collected my mother and we flew to Mobile, Alabama to visit them at a reunion of theirs in 2003. As I listened to stories of crew members, I felt something that I could not ever really experience, the bond that starts, grows and exists between shipmates. The ship is long gone, but the bond that existed between those veterans still was and is vibrant. We went to visit the LST 325 being restored to wartime condition there at the time in 2003. LST 325 has glory of her own; she had been at the Normandy invasion June 6, 1944. Being bought from the Greek Navy she sailed again across the Atlantic to Mobile, an epic in its own right. The 325 gave me a sense of what these magnificent amphibious ships had been like. They are very large. The old crew of 791 still knew and talked about their stations on the 325, as if she was the 791. If you ever get a chance to visit 325, I would encourage you to do so. It will be worthwhile and you will honor the men who sailed the LSTs into combat. The 325 is now berthed as a memorial and museum in Evansville Indiana. These men, ships and other craft of the alligator navy, as they have been known, had been every bit as vital, maybe more so, to winning the war in the Pacific and the Atlantic. Without the LSTs and their crews the troops, tanks, ammunition, fuel and other supplies to fight the war would not have been possible, nor would have victory. These men did a job, not as glamorous, but they delivered the goods, fighting to defend their ships and cargo and even dying if necessary in the process. This story is in their honor and memory.

One of the proudest moments in my life is when the surviving members of LST 791 made me an honorary member of their association and crew.

Arriving at LST 325 in Mobile Bay (Stripe).

Going on board LST 325 (Stripe)

Looking toward the Conn from the bow on the
main deck of LST 325 (Stripe).

In the Conn at the wheel (Stripe).

In the Conn explaining their duties and function of equipment (Stripe).

*In the tank deck of LST 325. Fern Stripe-Bruhn is facing
away in the fore ground walking through the tank deck with
791 crew members and one of the Spouses (Stripe).*

Bow Ramp (Stripe)

Aft part of the tank deck. Note the Greek flag as she was recently purchased from the Greek Navy (Stripe).

Traffic control station on the port side of the tank deck forward (Stripe).

Large stern wench for getting the ship off the beach(Stripe).

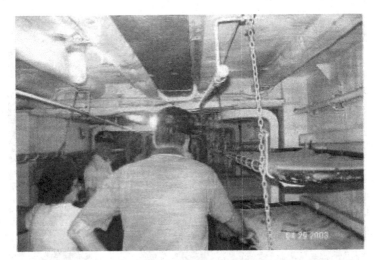

Quarters for casuals along the tank deck (Stripe).

Going through the navigation/radio room (Stripe).

One of LST 791 black gang crew members (Thomas L. Lane) in the engine room of LST 325, 2003 (Stripe).

LST 791 Association crew with wives. Author and Fern L. Stripe- Bruhn is third from the right. Thomas Lane and his daughter Maureen, James Hill and his wife, Charlie Haight and his wife, Harold Lohr and his wife, R. M. Sullivan (Sully) and his wife, John Burdnick and his wife, Clarence Blair and his wife, and Phillip Oaks and his wife (Stripe).

APPENDIX

Names in bold are commanders, men with particular stories, men whose diaries I had access to and men who I interviewed.

Deck Log: Wed, 27 September, 1944

Officers and Enlisted Personnel During Commissioning Ceremonies:
Officers;
Commanding Officer; Lt. **Andrew Duncan**
Executive Officer; Lt. .jg. Edward M. Horton
First Lieutenant; **Lt. j.g. Reed L. Adams**
Engineering Officer; **Lt. j.g. Carles J. Berlau**
Gunnery Officer; Ens. Ralph R. Bohrer
Communications Officer; Ens. Wladlslav J. Zizik
Supply Officer; Lt. j.g. Harold T. Durkin
Enlisted Personnel;

Abbott, Francis J. - S1c	Allison, George G - F2c
Almy, Bryant L - M2c	Anderson, James C - S2c
Anderson, Robert L - CBM A	Angermann, F O - S1c SC
Baker, Melvin - MoMM3c	Baker, Richard W - RM3c
Bani, John A -Cox	Barcewski, A. C. - MoMM3c
Barron, John H - S2c	Bass, Joseph T. - RM3c
Beatty, Russell L. - S1c	Beckmann, George W. – S1c
Bednarz, Casimir J. - S1c	**Blair, Clarence W - F1c EM**

Bohler, Hugo A. - S1c

Budnick, John M - S1c

Burdick, Raymond E - CM1c

Cerajewski, Edw. J. - S2c

Charbonnet, J. A. - BM2c

Cramer, Renell J. – GM3c

Cutler, James E. – StM3c

Dawson, John W. – S2c

Doherty, Owen P. – S1c

Donnelly, C. J. – GM1c

Downham, Robert W.– MoMM2c

Dwork, George – S2c

Eccleston, Louis A. – S2c

Farrow, Robert Jr. – S2c

Finger, Charles W. – GM3c

Frank, George W. Jr. – AS

Griffin, Harold J. – F1c

Hansen, William H. – GM3c

Hill, James E. – F1c

Keck, Charles W. – MoMM1c

Lane, Thomas J. – MoMM1c

Lohr, Harold R. – S1c SM

Maloney, Richard C. – S2c

McMahon, Gordon F. – S2c

Mestre, Caesar – S2c

Morley, James E. – PhM2c

Musser, Francis M. – BM2c

Oaks, Phillip A. – EM2c

Poppino, William H. – S2c

Prescott, F. F. – S1c

Puscar, Carter M. – F2c

Reiser, Edward F. – S2c

Breitzman, Marvin - MoMM2c

Burn, Francis M. - S1c

Carpenter T. H. - S1c

Chandler, Kenneth - MoMM1c

Clark, Lloyd G. - F1c

Crowe, Robert H. – StM3c

Czerniak, Chester – StM3c

Delgado, Miguel A. – S2c

Dolan, Raymond L. – S2c

Douglass, Howard W. – GM3c

Dulemba, Henry A – GM3c

Earll, Morris H. – CmoMM T

Eisenberg, Myron D. – S2c

Fernandez, Victor – S1c

Forbus, Donald B. – SC2c

Graham, Charles B. – GM1c

Haight, Charles L. – MoMM2c

Higgins, C H Jr. – CmoMM

Joyce, Eugene F – S1c FC

LaFountain, R J. - MoMM2c

Leininger, R J. – S2c

MacLean, Karl S. – SM3c

Marlow, Elbert W. – MoMM2c

Meshurel, Russell R. – GM3c

Miesen, Donald B. – S2c

Motola, Leon – S1c

Myers, William H. – S2c

Pinckney, Ambrose J. – CM1c

Poyner, Urias D. – SC2c

Price, James E. – S1c

Reid, William, L. – F2c

Richards, Robert M. S2c RDM

Riley, Howard J. – Y2c
Rowland, Marvin D. – F1c WT
Schierer, John E. – MoMM3c
Segaritis, Frank J. – F2c
Shane, Joseph C. – MoMM3c
Sliger, Gilbert L. – S1c
Smith, Lawrence E. – F1c MoM
Specht, Edward X. – SC2c
Stripe, Max E. – S1c
Sullivan, R. M. Jr. – S1c
Sweeney, Richard T. – S1c
Thomas, Rufus M. – S2c
Thornhill, Billy – F2c
Tinker, Zack H – S1c
Waites, Stacey C. – S1c
Watt, Thomas G. – S1c
Wilson, Merle S. – CQM

Roeder, Carl O. – RM3c
Sanchez, Dilar – PhM3c
Schlernitzauer, R. F. – BM1c
Serridge, Edward – S1c
Skinner, Billy O. E. – S1c SC
Smith, Gilbert Jr. – S1c
Snay, Edward J. Jr. – S2c
Standfast, Milton – F1c WT
Stripp, Walter M. – S1c
Suminski, Leon M. – S2c
Talkin, Bernard J. – SK2c
Thompson, Hugh L. – F1c
Tiegs, Leroy H. – S1c
Vasquez, George – CCStd
Wallace, Minott T. Jr. – PhM1c
Weaver, Robert F. – S1c
Wood, Robert L. – Cox

Nash, Clyde – AS transferred off the crew Sept. 20 1944
Reported Aboard September 29, 1944.
Lt (jg) Frank C Ruppert- Recognition Officer
Lt. (jg) James E. Bradford – Recognition Officer
Reported aboard as of 5 October 1944

Carey, Richard W. – S Ic
Viollis, Michael – S1c

Lundin, Richard C. – SC3c

Reported for duty 30 October, 1944

Courtmanoge, Roland A. – St.M.3c
McMeecham, John V. – F2c
Werschler, Thomas – S1c
Yunkin, W. J. – F1c

Ivey, Noble B.
Smith, LeRoy C. – RT3c
Yetka, F. X. –S2c

Crew not on Sept 1944 Roster that joined later to replace others transferred after October 30 1944 through December 31, 1945.

Woolfrey, Clarence I	Harrison, John K.
Maclean, Karl S. – SM3c	**Dime, Marvin –F1c,**
Dekar, Walter J. – FC3c	Gonzales, Thomas – S1c
Violis, Michael	Wilson, Jack – Lt.
Peetz, R. D. –S2c	Tibbols, M. E. –S1c
Pritchett, J. -Lt.	Wilson, J. - Lt.
Velvendy, B. V. –AS	Neugebauer, J. M. –AS
Omlin, D. M. –AS	Lang, H. J. –F2c
Lankin, E. L. –AS	O'Malley, P. O. –AS
Pryor, W. G. –AS	Kaniss, H. A. – Lt. (dentist)
Steele, D. C. –S1c	Benolken, D. J. – Ens.
Daughtry, A. L. – Lt.	Jensen, J. E. – RM3c

Others reported aboard from January 1946 through to decommissioning while in dock in San Francisco, as others were discharged.

Deck Log for April 1, 1945

0400 to 0800

Anchored off Okinawa Island in twenty-eight (28) fathoms of water to six hundred (600) feet of cable on the stern anchor.

0800 to 1200

Anchored as before.

0828- Debarkation completed. The following Marine officers and men of the Second Battalion, 22nd Regiment departed, transportation completed.

Dayes, Frank, 1st Lt.	Hambright, A. B.	Flaherty, jR. J.
Deer, Jas, D., 2nd Lt.	Hartman, J. M.	Frazier, B. C.
Meeks, T. A.	Hildebrand T. L.	Gordon, B. C.
Greene, J. S.	Hixenbaugh, C. W.	Gordon, M. A.
Trzeciakiewicz, A.	Koch, J.	Gott, A. T.

Jones, R. A.	Medintz, C. C.	Gould, W. H.
Neltner, R. H.	Omiatek, E.	Grant, H. E.
Smith, J. P.	Amonette, R. L. Lt.(jg)	Haag, J. C.
Williams, E. M.	Carnahan, H.L. Lt.(jg)	Harrison, C. M.
Andrzejewski, Z.B.	**Woodhouse, H.C.Jr. Lt.Col.**	Hart, J. E.
Basile, R. T.	Martin, G.E. Major	Hilliard, R. A.
Boals, J.B.	Deal,J.C.Capt.	Jong, B. L.
Boyd, L.G.	Miller, D.E. 1st Lt.	Loag, W.J.
Cheney, N.H.	O'Connell, J.J. 1st Lt.	Martin, J. W.
Damon, E. H.	Swindal,F.L.1st Lt.	Mathews, T.J. Jr.
Jarels, H.W.	Harris,R.E.,2nd Lt.	McCulloch, J.,Jr.
Mayeran, W.	Sutton,J.R.,2nd Lt.	McDanel., D.
Moore, J.C.	Mihalak,S.J.	McNally,J.C.
Scott, J.A.	Allen, W. W.	Mohler, C. D.
Turner, J. G. Jr.	Thomas, R. G.	Moore, H. R.
Warren, J. C.	Bailey, E. G.	Neill, O. E. Sr.
Wellenkotter, E. K.	Kemp, D. M.	Neuhart, R. F.
Baxter, L. H.	Burden, J. B.	Notte, G. A.
Beaudry, S. A.	Cofer, D.	Palmer, R. A.
Brooks, H. R.	Corey, R. A.	Perkins, R. W.
Bruns, R. H.	Ham, P.	Poer, K. w.
Byrd, C. S.	Heard, W. H.	Rogan, J. L.
Carothers, T. M.	Hern, W. O.	Root, T. J.
Casto, A. W.	Leach, R. J.	Solberg, L.C.
Clevenger, D.W.	Lipes, C.D.Jr.	Stinton, B. A.
Duffy, T. H.	McAlister, A. E.	Thomas, R. L.
Essa, W.L.	Rogers, W. B.	Ursich, S. Jr.
Folsom, E. E.	Wright, R. G.	Webster, H. W.
Isaacs, A. H.	Adams, G. H.	White, J. W. Jr.

Jones, J. T.

Livingston, F. R.

Beall, M. F. Jr. 1st Lt.

O'Grady, J. J. Jr.

Altamirano, A. J.

Colvin, R.L.

Holt, R. L.

Johnson, R. E.

King, H. T.

Mangum, G. L. Jr.

Quetschenback, R. N.

Weise, E. J., Jr.

Bramschreiber, H. E.

Davis, O., Jr.

Mitchell, J. C.

Newhouse, W. H.

Newman, M.

Sheehy, J. B. Jr.

Fleck,R.L. Lt.(jg)

Vallon, R.

Clark, B.

Haller, A. J.

Watkins, E.R.

Webb, K. L.

Falk, G. J.

Jordan, S.

Kleeger, S.

Miller, W. R.

Potter, D. C.

Welcher, R. D.

Andonian, L. S.

Asay, W. F.

Balisciano, J. A.

Barciay, F. J. Jr.

Bassford, B. E.

Bauer, E. S.

Bofto, E. C.

Bisio, R. P.

Breisch, C. C.

Boudreau, J. L.

Butler, J. P.

Clay, N.

Cutler, R. T.

Dunn, B. A.

Kelly, C.

Makousky, M. R.

Mazzola, J. J., Jr.

McCain, R. O.

McDaniel, R. J.

Ostboe, K.L.

Osterman, J. F.

Owens, D. T.

Roberts, A. L. R.

Lebahain, E. L.

Bair, D.W., 1st Lt.

Stevens, J. A. 1st Lt.

Maresh, P. C.

Habern, F. Jr.

Goslowski, A. F.

Brown, J. C.

Lovell, J. E.

McLaughlin, G. H.

Angerhauser, W. A.

Barrett, M. V.

Bartlomejczik, M.J.

Batdorf, F.

Beall, F. L.

Beard, A. M.

Gilker, J. A.

Knepper, F. A.

McDonell, L. D.

McRae, D.

Merrion, E. P. Jr.

Miller, H. C.

Kumpf, C. M.

Stewart, J. A., 2nd Lt.

Jackman, C. J.

Lotz, G. D.

McGookin, A. G.

Meyer, F. F.

Morgan, D. E.

Morlock, R. C.

Pienta, F. T.

Thibaul, J. E.

Parker, A. H.

Summers, C. C.

Morgan, J. E.

Twitty, H. W.

Tashjian, K. V. 2nd Lt.

Peterson, V. E.

Pesely, E. H.,1st Lt.
Flynn, M. E. 2nd Lt.
Gaumnitz, R.E.
2nd Lt.
Gagat, S.
McCollum, R.E.
Grubb, G. A.
Prezzano, R. W.
Abrahams, N. E.
Genakos, H. S.
Hall, L. D.
Holliday, M. M.
Kereszturi, E. J.
Kivett, A. L.
Leo, J. E.
Lesmeister, P.
Pavalko, G. E.
Roberson, W. G.
Aldous, M. C.
Cassidy, J. J.
Crisanti, A. D.
Dornick, J.
Elwood, J. A.
Finkbeiner, R. H.
Flosom, N. F.
Fontaine, A. J.
Garcia, D.
Greenwood, L. P. Jr.
Judd, F. J.
Kahle, E. W.
Kaltenbrown, G. F.
Kastler, E. L.

Budzinski, W.
Bullin, H.
Butcher, I.L.

Catania, C. J.
Ellis, W. T.
Headrick, R. E.
Porter, R. Jr.
Smith, J. E.
Stankovich, S.
Blair, F. J.
Bowers, J. F.
Bruhn, C. J.
Calhoun, T. S.
Campanella, J. L.
Capalare, D. G.
Dereschuk, D.
Desher, J. T.
Durbin, O.
Erickson, J. P. Jr.
Faver, W. R.
Gallegos, L. S.
Henry, E. N.
Herb, M. Jr.
Herring, M. B.
Jordan, L. F.
Morgan, W. F.
Monaco, S.
Musgrove, J. W.
Otzenberger, J.
Parsons, E.
Pfortmiller, W. H.

Miller, H. Jr.
Hristiansecn, L. G.
Staley, P. I.

Franznik, W. J.
Mogilsky, J. W.
Becker, G. P. Jr.
Bertoli, D. C.
Boeke, C. H.
Felix, R. F.
Henry, C. A. Jr.
Jovaag, J. P.
Prowant, D. E.
Simpson, W. G.
Stines, C. E. Jr.
Thompson, M. G.
Jennings, L. R.
Gilbert, E. S.
Lundquist, M. C.
Machowski, E. J.
Manley, M. C.
Mauzey, E. F.
McCarty, J. G.
Birstol, C. P.
Evancek, R.
Day, J. L.
Cash, R. M.
Marascola, A. F.
Schroffraneck, W. F.
Young, R. F.
Barnett, D. E. 2nd Lt.
Quinet, J. J. Lt (jg)

King, B. A.	Savage, R. J.	Smith, T. J.
Leonard, P. M.	Tew, E. Jr.	Harrington, W. H.
Low, K. M.	Young, E. G.	McGray, G. W.
Nuyianes, J. S.	McCall, J. W.	Barnes, L. A. Jr.
Odom, S. H.	Haag, E. M.	Kirkman, P.
Paquette, W. J.	Jedra, F. D.	Nicks, W. R.
Perry, K. C.	Jones, R. E.	Toothaker, N. E.
Pierman, D. H.	Joyner, J. W.	Wallace, J. c.
Spencer, M. G.	Juse, D. W.	Slesnick, I. L.
Ward, G.	Kelly, W. E. R.	Lindsay, C. S. 1st Lt.
Zellner, F. M.	Kishish, G. W.	Alicea, W.
Zubal, S. Jr.	Koonce, W. M.	Woodard, W. D., Sr.
Buss, E. R.	Langston, R. L.	Blackston, B. H.
Capeau, E. R.	Mullooly, G. D.	Ferdio, J. M.
Daddario, M. E.	Papp, J. G. Jr.	Funaro, R. P.
Del Cioppo, V. J.	Parinello, J.	Pierce, J. E.
Fish, D. A.	Slavicek, F. R.	Uressman, D.
Gleason, A.	Hanlin, R. E.	Schuhart, R. C.
Johnson, E. A.		

Deck Log 2 April, 1945

8-12

Anchored as before.

0827 – Launched starboard pontoon causeway.

Making preparations to launch LCT

12-16

Anchored as before.

1200 – Pontoon causeways towed from ship.

Lt. N. E. MacDougall, CEC, USNR, and the following Seabees departed, transportation completed.

Ray, Angus M. CMM
Bath, Chas, H. Jr. CM2c
Bush, Leroy W. MM2c
Despain, Paul A. MM2c
Fairbanks, Harold J. WT2c
Howard, Curtis E. MM2c
Keith, Willie T. MM2c
Rapp, Henry J. MM2c
Morrison, John H. CM1c
Patterson, Oliver G. MM3c
Rester, George H. MM2c

Bartlett, Raymond I. S2c
Brasier, Jas. G. MMS2c
Calabrese, Lawrence W. S2c
Dent, Clarence W. Jr. MMS2c
Herring, Glenwood MM2c
Kaminiski, Frank J. MM2c
Locklin, Claude E. S2c
Montoya, Manuel G. SF3c
Nelson, Ernest C. MM2c
Stoligts, Frank M. MM2c
Riddlesbarger, Claude D. PhM2c

Deck Log 3 April, 1945

Anchored off Okinawa Island, White Beach, in thirty three fathoms of water with 325 feet of cable to stern anchor. 0015- Commenced fueling LCT 828.

0210- Completed fueling LCT 828, 3450 gallons of fuel transferred.

0215- LCT – 828 departed with the following officers and men, transportation completed.

Rockett, E. S. U.S.N.R. Ensign
Boyd, Leon, MOMM 3c(T)
Hagen, Robert, S2c
Heath, James W. S1c
Leonard, Raymond O. BM2c
McLaughlin, Francis J. EM3c
Munn, Elmer L. S2c
Reed, Chas. H. GM3c
Wolcott, Robert S1c
Maupin, H. W. SC3c

Rodgers, F. L. U.S.N.R. Ensign
Gale, Lloyd E. Jr. S1c
Hardy, Raymond B. QM3c
Koehler, Henry E. S1c (RM)
Lovelace, George W. S2c
Morris, Frank H. S2c
Pastura, Anthony L. S1c
Robbins, Martin Jr. SC2c
Isby, Harvey S. Cox

States of Origin of Crew Members of Sept. 1944.

Alabama – 1	California – 7	Colorado – 2
Connecticut – 1	Florida – 3	Georgia – 1
Illinois – 5	Indiana – 1	Iowa – 2
Kansas – 2	Kentucky – 2	Louisiana – 4
Maryland – 4	Massachusetts – 9	Michigan – 7
Minnesota – 2	Missouri – 2	New Jersey – 10
New York – 25	Ohio – 8	Oklahoma – 4
Oregon – 1	Pennsylvania – 8	Rhode Island – 1
S. Carolina – 2	N. Dakota – 1	Tennesse – 1
Texas – 6	Vemont – 1	Virginia – 3
Washington – 1	Washington D.C. -3	Wisconsin – 3

CHRONOLOGY:

Places, Dates and Distances Traveled Since Commissioning;

Sept 16, 1944- Departed Pittsburgh for New Orleans 1800 miles

Oct 28, 1944- Left for Mobile Alabama, picked up 850 tons of ammunition

November 1, 1944- Left for Colon, Panama 1450 miles

November 8, 1944 – arrived in Panama City, Panama after traveling the canal length of 44 miles

November 10, 1944- Departed Panama for San Diego Calif. 2843 miles.

November 25, 1944- Left San Diego for Pearl Harbor 2885 miles.

December 30, 1944- Left Pearl Harbor for Eniwetok in the Marshall Islands 2823 miles.

January 4-5, 1945- Crossed the International Date Line

January 7, 1945- Passed Kwajalein island.

January 9, 1945- Arrived at Eniwetok.

January 10-, 1945- Started for Babelthaup in the Palau islands 1726 miles.

January 20, 1945- Convoy split at Ulithi.

January 22, 1945- Arrived at Babelthaup.

January 27, 1945- Departed for Tacloban, Leyte, Philippines 622 miles.

February 2, 1945, arrived in the Philippines, unloaded troops and ammunition.

February 8, 1945- Set sail for Guadalcanal, Solomon Islands 2500 miles.

February 13, 1945- Crossed the Equator.

February 19, 1945- Arrived at Guadalcanal.

March 12, 1945- Left for Ulithi 1800 miles.

March 21, 1945- Departed for Okinawa 1300 miles.

April 1, 1945- Invasion of Okinawa.

April 6, 1945- Shot down kamikaze.

April 10, 1945- Left for Saipan in the Mariana's 1300 miles

April 17, 1945- Arrived in Saipan.

May 3, 1945- Left Saipan for Guam 130 miles.

May 4, 1945- Arrived at Guam and loaded 1200 tons of ammunition.

May 9, 1945- Back to Saipan 130 miles.

May 12, 1945- Left for Okinawa 1300 miles.

May 19, 1945- Arrived at Okinawa.

May 31, 1945- Departed Okinawa for Ie Shima.

June 8, 1945- Okinawa largest air raids, 38 raids in 24 hours. 135 Bogey contacts.

June 11, 1945- Left for Kerama Rhetto.

June 12, 1945- Back to Okinawa.

June 13, 1945- Left for Iheya.

June 14, 1945- Arrived at Iheya and departed for Aguna.

June 17, 1945- Arrived at Aguna.

June 18, 1945- Left Aguna for Okinawa.

June 22, 1945- Left for Leyte, Philippines. 1020 miles.

June 27, 1945- Arrived at Leyte.

July 8, 1945- Left for Cebu, Philippines 275 miles.

July 9, 1945- Arrived at Cebu.

July 22, 1945- Departed for Lucena city 500 miles.

July 24, 1945- Arrived in Lucena city.

August 15, 1945- Departed for Subic Bay 400 miles

August 16, 1945- Arrived at Subic Bay.

August 26, 1945- Left for Manila and arrived 200 miles.

September 3, 1945- Departed for Tokyo, Japan 1790 miles.

September 12, 1945- Arrived at Tokyo.

Left Tokyo for Leyte 1743 miles.

Leyte for Cebu 275 miles.

Cebu for Leyte 275 miles.

Leyte to Otsu Hokkaido Japan 2460 miles.

Otsu Hokkaido to Hokdate, Hokkaido Japan 250 miles.

Hokodate to Yokohama 700 miles.

Yokama to Saipan, Marianas 1500 miles.

Saipan to Pearl Harbor 3600 miles.

Pearl Harbor to San Francisco arriving on March 15, 1946 2200miles.

LST 791 carried a combat load worth $1,300,000.00. Total cargo carried estimated worth $6,700,000.00 as of June 1, 1945,

Landing Craft and Transport Characteristics:

LST 791

Displacement: 1,625 tons empty (light), 4,080 tons loaded
Length: 327 ft 9 in.
Beam: 50 ft.
Draft: 1 ft. 6 in. bow, 7 ft. 5 in. stern; unloaded
    8 ft. 2 in. bow, 14 ft. 1 in. stern; loaded at sea
    3 ft. 1 in. bow, 9 ft. 6 in. stern; loaded beach
Speed: 11.6 knots, top; Cruising 9 knots
Crew: 7 officers, 75-111 enlisted
Troops: 163
Cargo: 1,900 tons,
Tanks: 20 Sherman's or 17 LVT's
Boats: 2 LCVP
Armament: 7 x 40mm, 6x 20 mm, 2x .50 cal. Mgs, 4 x .30 cal. Mgs

APA 71 USS Catron (Gilliam Class) Attack Transport

Displacement: 4,247 tons
Length: 426 ft.
Beam: 58 ft.
Draft: 16 ft.
Speed: 16.9 knots
Cargo: 600 tons
Crew: 27 officers, 295 enlisted
Troops: 47 officers, 802 enlisted
Armament: 1x 5 in., 8 x 40 mm, 10 x 20 mm

LCI Landing Craft Infantry

Displacement: 234 tons empty, 389 tons loaded
Length: 158 ft. 6 in.
Beam: 23 ft. 3 in.
Draft: 5 ft. 4 in. bow, 5 ft. 11 in. stern
Speed: 16 knots
Crew: 3 officers, 21 enlisted
Troops: 180
Armament: 4 x 20 mm

Landing Ship Medium

Displacement: 530 tons empty, 900 tons loaded
Length: 203 ft. 6 in.
Beam: 34 ft.
Draft: 3 ft. 6 in forward, 7 ft. 8 in. stern empty
    6 ft. 4 in. forward, 8 ft. 3 in. stern loaded
Speed: 13 knots
Crew: 4 officers, 54 enlisted
Cargo: 5 Sherman tanks or 6 LVT or 9 DUKW or 54 troops
Armament: 2 x 40 mm, 4 x 20 mm

Landing Craft Support [Large]

Displacement: 250 tons
Length: 158 ft. 6 in.
Beam: 23 ft. 3 in.
Draft: 5 ft. 10 in.
Range: 5,500 miles
Speed: 16.5 knots
Crew: 3-6 officers, 55-68 enlisted

Armament: 1x 3 in, Twin 40 mm or single 40 mm in the bow, 2 x 40 Mm Twin deck guns, 4x 20mm, 4 x .50 cal mgs, 10x MK 7 rocket Launcher

Armor: 10 lbs STS Splinter

Landing Craft Tank (Type VI) 828

Displacement: 143 tons empty, 309 tons loaded
Length: 119 ft.
Beam: 32 ft.
Draft: 3 ft. 7 in. forward, 4 ft. aft loaded
Speed: 8 knots
Crew: 1 officer, 12 enlisted
Cargo: 4 Sherman tanks, or 150 tons of cargo
Armament: 2 x 20 mm.

LCM (Landing Craft Mechanized), 8 variants

Weight: 35 tons
Length: 45 ft.
Beam: 14 ft.
Draft: 13 ft.
Speed: 8 knots
Armament: two .50 cal. M2 machine guns
Crew: 4-5
Cargo: 30 ton tank (M4 Sherman), 60 troops, 60,000 lbs

LCVP (Landing Craft Vehicle Personnel)

Weight: 18,000 lbs.
Length: 36 ft. 3 in.
Beam: 10 ft. 10 in.
Draft: 2 ft. 2 in., 3 ft. loaded

Speed: 12 knots
Crew: 3
Cargo: 1 x 6,000 vehicle or 8,100 lbs. cargo
Troops: 36
Armament: 2 x .30 cal. Mgs

LVT (Landing Vehicle Tracked)

Weight: 16.5 tons
Length: 23.8 ft.
Width: 9.7f ft.
Crew: 3-4
Troops: 36
Armament: 2 x .30 cal. Mgs

USS Comfort (AH-6)

Displacement: 6,000 tons
Length: 417 ft. 9 in.
Beam: 60 ft.
Speed: 14 knots
Complement: 233
Patient Capacity: 700
Armament: none

REFERENCES

Adams, Reed USCG (Ret.), *The Men on USCG LST 791*; unpublished

Blair, Clarence W., crewman LST 791, 2003 interview.

BLUEJACKETS' MANUAL 1940, 10th Ed. United States Naval Institute, Annapolis, Maryland 1940.

Browning Jr., Robert M.; *The Coast Guard at Okinawa*, United States Coast Guard, U. S. Department of Homeland Security.

Deck Log LST 791 1944-46.

Dictionary of American Naval Fighting Ships Vol. VII; James L. Mooney Ed. *Naval Historical Center Department of the Navy*, Washington; 1981

Dime, Marvin; *War Diary;* 1945, unpublished.

Feifer, George, *The Battle of Okinawa The Blood and the Bomb*; The

Lyons Press, Guilford, CT 2001

Gandt, Robert, *The Twilight Warriors;* Broadway Books, New York, 2010

Haight, Charles L., crewman LST 791, 2003 interview

Hallas, James H., *Killing Ground on Okinawa The Battle for Sugar Loaf Hill;* Naval Institute Press, Annapolis Md, 1996, 2007

Harper, Dale P.; *Too close for Comfort;* Trafford Publishing, 2001.

Haswell, Homer; *LSTs: The Ships with the Big Mouth,* Xlibris Corporation, 2005

Hill, James E., crewman LST 791, 2003 interveiw

Johnson, Robert Erwin, *Coast Guard-Manned Naval Vessels in World War II;* Coast Guard Historians Office and Commandants Bulletin, February 1993.

Knox, James W., *The Birth of the LST;* The Pennsylvania LST Association, 2000

Lacey, Laura Homan, *Stay Off the Skyline, The Sixth Marine Division on Okinawa,* Potomac Books, Inc. Washington D.C. 2005.

Thomas J. Lane, crewman LST 791, 2003 interview.

Leckie, Robert, *Okinawa the Last Battle of World War II;* Penguin Group, 1995.

LST Group 8, Action Report 1945

Martinez, Daniel; *West Loch Disaster,* Chapter II Historical Record; USS Arizona Memorial: 27 April 2001.

McConnell, Malcolm, *Hero of Sugar Loaf Hill;* Readers Digest, December 1998.

McGee, William L. *The Amphibians Are Coming! Emergence of the 'Gator Navy and its Revolutionary Landing Craft*. BMC Publications, 2000

Miller, Lee G., *The Story of Ernie Pyle;* Viking Press 1950

Morley, James E., crewman LST, 2003-2005 correspondence.

Naval Amphibious Base Little Creek; GlobalSecurity.org/military/facility/little_creek.htm. August 21, 2005.

Noble, Dennis L., *The Beach Patrol and Corsair Fleet;* Coast Guard Historians Office and Commandants Bulletin, March 1992.

Ostrom, Thomas P. *The United States Coast Guard in World War II, A History of Domestic and Overseas Actions;* McFarland & Company Inc. Publishers 2009

Pyle, Richard. "After 63 years, death photo of famed WWII reporter Ernie Pyle surfaces", The Seattle Times, Associated Press, 2008-02-13

Reilly, Robin L.; *Kamikaze Attacks of World War II, A Complete History of Japanese Suicide Strikes on American Ships, by Aircraft and Other Means;* McFarland & Company, Inc., Publishers, 2010.

Riley, Howard J.; *War Diary, Book 1 and Book 2;* 1944-45, unpublished.

Rottman, Gordon L., *Classic Battles, Okinawa 1945;* Osprey Publishing 2002

Rottman, Gordon L. *Landing Ship, Tank (LST) 1942-2002,* Osprey Publishing, 2008

Sherrod, Robert. "*World: Play That Failed.*" TIME Magazine, 16, April 1945.

Stripe-Bruhn Fern L., wife of Max E. Stripe 2003-2010 interview/ papers

Sullivan, R. M., crewman LST 791, 2003 inteview.

Tobin, James, "*Ernie Pyle's War, America's Eyewitness to World War 2*"; Free Press, New York London Toronto Sydney, 1997

Weaver, Robert; War Diary; 1944-45 unpublished.

Wiley, Ken. "*D-Days In the Pacific With the U.S. Coast Guard, The Story of Lucky 13*"; CASEMATE, Havertown, PA, 2010

Witter, Robert E. *Small Boats and Large Slow Targets; Oral Histories of the United States Amphibious Forces Personnel in WWII.* Pictorial Histories Publishing Co. Inc., 1998.

Lt. Commander Andrew Duncan's Memoirs, with permission of

Isabel D. Hatchet, Madeleine D. Hughes (daughters of A. Duncan), 1945.

Unpublished.

Printed in the United States
by Baker & Taylor Publisher Services